Resilient
Playgrounds

Beth Doll with **Katherine Brehm**

Routledge
Taylor & Francis Group
New York   London

Routledge
Taylor & Francis Group
270 Madison Avenue
New York, NY 10016

Routledge
Taylor & Francis Group
27 Church Road
Hove, East Sussex BN3 2FA

Printed in the United States of America on acid-free paper
10 9 8 7 6 5 4 3 2 1

International Standard Book Number: 978-0-415-96087-8 (Hardback) 978-0-415-96088-5 (Paperback)

Library of Congress Cataloging-in-Publication Data

Doll, Beth, 1952-
   Resilient playgrounds / Beth J. Doll.
      p. cm.
   Includes bibliographical references and index.
   ISBN 978-0-415-96087-8 (hardcover : alk. paper) -- ISBN 978-0-415-96088-5 (pbk. : alk. paper)
      1. Playgrounds--Psychological aspects. 2. Playgrounds--Social aspects. 3. Student counseling. 4. Playgrounds--Safety measures. I. Title.

LB3251.D65 2009
372.1801'9--dc22
                                                                    2009017880

Visit the Taylor & Francis Web site at
http://www.taylorandfrancis.com

and the Routledge Web site at
http://www.routledgementalhealth.com

Resilient

Playgrounds

Routledge
Taylor & Francis Group

SCHOOL-BASED PRACTICE IN ACTION SERIES

Series Editors
Rosemary B. Mennuti, Ed.D., NCSP
and
Ray W. Christner, Psy.D., NCSP
Philadelphia College of Osteopathic Medicine

This series provides school-based practitioners with concise practical guidebooks that are designed to facilitate the implementation of evidence-based programs into school settings, putting the best practices *in action*.

PUBLISHED TITLES

Implementing Response-to-Intervention in Elementary and Secondary Schools: Procedures to Assure Scientific-Based Practices
Matthew K. Burns and Kimberly Gibbons

Assessment and Intervention for Executive Function Difficulties
George McCloskey, Lisa A. Perkins, and Bob Van Divner

Resilient Playgrounds
Beth Doll

FORTHCOMING TITLES

Comprehensive Planning for Safe Learning Environments: A School Counselor's Guide to Integrating Physical and Psychological Safety—Prevention through Recovery
Melissa A. Reeves, Amy E. Plog, and Linda M. Kanan

Behavioral Interventions in Schools: A Response-to-Intervention Guidebook
David Hulac, Joy Terrell, Odell Vining, and Joshua Bernstein

Serving the Gifted: Evidence-Based Clinical and Psycho-Educational Practice
Steven I. Pfeiffer

Ecobehavioral Consultation in Schools: Theory and Practice for School Psychologists, Special Educators, and School Counselors
Steven W. Lee

A Guide to Psychiatric Services in Schools: Understanding Roles, Treatment, and Collaboration
Shawna S. Brent

The Power of Partnering Families and Schools: A Comprehensive Resource for School Mental Health Professionals and Educators
Cathy Lines, Gloria Miller, and Amanda Arthur

Comprehensive Children's Mental Health Services in Schools and Communities
Rick Jay Short and Robyn S. Hess

Everyday Program Evaluation for Schools: Implementation and Outcomes
Diane Smallwood and Susan G. Forman

Pediatric School Psychology: Conceptualization, Applications, and Leadership Development
Thomas J. Power and Kathy L. Bradley-Klug

Contents

List of Figures and Tables

Series Editors' Foreword

The *School-Based Practice in Action* series grew out of the coming together of our passion and commitment to the field of education and the needs of children and schools in today's world. We entered the process of developing and editing this series at two different points of our career, though both in phases of transition. One (RWC) moving from the opening act to the main scene and the other (RBM) from main scene to the final act. Despite one of us entering the peak of action and the other leaving it, we both continue to be faced with the same challenges in and visions for education and serving children and families.

Significant transformations to the educational system, through legislation such as the *No Child Left Behind Act* and the reauthorization of *Individuals with Disabilities Education Act* (IDEA 2004), have brought about broad sweeping changes for the practitioners in the educational setting, and these changes will likely continue. It is imperative that as school-based practitioners we maintain a strong knowledge base and adjust our service delivery. To accomplish this, there is a need to understand theory and research, but it is critical that we have resources to move our empirical knowledge into the process of practice. Thus, it is our goal that the books included in the *School-Based Practice in Action* series truly offer resources for readers to put directly "into action."

To accomplish this, each book in the series will offer information in a practice-friendly manner and will have a companion CD with reproducible and usable materials. Within the text, readers will find a specific icon that will cue them to documents available on the accompanying CD. These resources are designed to have a direct impact on transitioning research and knowledge into the day-to-day functions of school-based practitioners. We recognize that the implementation of programs and the changing of roles come with challenges and barriers, and as such, these may take on various forms depending on the context of the situation and the voice of the practitioner. To that end, the books of the *School-Based Practice in Action* series may be used in their entirety and present form for a number of practitioners; however, for others, these books will help them find new ways to move toward effective action and new possibilities. No matter which style fits your practice, we hope that these books will influence your work and professional growth.

We are thrilled to have had the opportunity to work with Dr. Beth Doll and Dr. Katherine Brehm on our newest addition to the series. Doll and Brehm have developed an outstanding guidebook on an under-investigated, yet crucial topic that has always been at the heart of social learning for children — the playground. In this book, *Resilient Playgrounds*, Doll and Brehm have given us a problem-solving model for the development of strategies and interventions to use on school playgrounds that will promote social competence and social success. The wise minds and practical experience of the authors provide us with the tools to develop a healthy arena in which children and youth can develop growth-fostering peer relationships and social competence. This book goes beyond simply providing ideas around using the playground as a "place of learning" social competence, and it offers action steps for school-based practitioners to get involved. We applaud Doll and Brehm for their vision in extending school-based mental health and wellness services beyond the classroom and traditional mental health services. We hope that this book will be the start of many new resources focusing on ways to use less traditional times of the school day to augment social learning.

Finally, our vision of this book series would have never come to fruition without the ongoing support of Mr. Dana Bliss and Routledge Publishing. We are grateful for their belief in our idea of having a book series focusing on action resources dedicated to enriching practice and service delivery within school settings. Their openness to meet the needs of school-based practitioners made the *School-Based Practice in Action* series possible. We hope that you enjoy reading and implementing the materials in this book and the rest of the series as much as we have enjoyed working with the authors on developing these resources.

Rosemary B. Mennuti, EdD, NCSP
Ray W. Christner, PsyD, NCSP
Series Editors, School-Based Practice in Action Series

One

Introduction to Resilient Playgrounds

A special connection exists between students' social competence and the playgrounds that schools provide for them. Some of the social success that students experience can be attributed to the physical setting of the playground, the social climate created with their peers, and the caretaking environments that are fostered by school recess practices. Strengthening playground settings can be an important first step toward fostering students' social success and ultimately their social competence. These, then, are my two overarching goals for this book, *Resilient Playgrounds*: (a) to provide a conceptual framework for understanding playground contexts and their relation to students' social success, and (b) to articulate a strategy for assessing playgrounds, identifying features that might disrupt students' social interactions, intervening to modify these features, and monitoring to ensure that the interventions have led to more successful peer relationships. A central premise of the book is that the social competence of students will be more evident when school playgrounds support strong interpersonal relationships and self-regulated play.

Recess is an omnipresent part of the elementary school experience in the United States. In the early elementary grades, classes may have both morning and afternoon recess breaks, typically 10 to 20 minutes in length (Pellegrini, 2005). By the upper elementary grades, most classes have only one scheduled recess break, but almost every grade has a lunch recess in which students are dismissed to play for a brief period after eating their lunch. As recently as 10 years ago, 90% of the states reported that schools had these kinds of daily elementary school recess periods (Pellegrini, 1995).

The tacit assumption that school days should include recess is historical in origin (Moore, 2006). The playgrounds of the mid-1800s were intended to be instructional, and teachers would join students in playing games that explored the physical properties of objects in movement and at rest. By the early 1900s, large cities developed playgrounds to be safe havens where urban youth could play cooperatively and engage in healthy physical exercise away from urban traffic hazards. By the 1950s, most schools and community parks had paved playgrounds furnished with durable steel slides, swings, see-saws, merry-go-rounds, and jungle gyms. Many of these proto-typic playgrounds were dismantled as evidence accumulated that students were often injured when they ran into, fell from, jumped from, or were pinched by metal play structures. These have been replaced by playgrounds in naturalized settings, with custom play structures, and softer and safer designs and materials. Today's playgrounds have also been shaped by a renewed interest in the potential of play environments to foster cognitive growth and imaginative play.

Playgrounds are unique settings in many other respects. They are almost always large settings, larger than most students' yards or indoor classrooms or gymnasiums, and their size allows students to run, tumble, and jump faster, further, and for longer periods than in most other play settings. On most playgrounds, adult supervisors are fewer and further away, and supervision is less constant than in classrooms, youth clubs, or after-school day care centers (Pellegrini & Blatchford, 2000). As a result, the playground at recess is "one of the very few places in school where there is minimal adult direction, where students can interact with each other on their own terms" (Pellegrini & Blatchford, 2000, p. 21).

Because their social competence is incompletely developed, peer interactions can be a struggle for students when they negotiate their own play with very limited adult direction. Problems with peer aggression and conflict are frequent. In my own work with Midwestern elementary schools, 22% of elementary students reported that kids in their class *almost always* or *often* argue with each other, and call each other names (Doll, 2008; Doll, Kurien, et al., 2009). As will be explained in Chapter 2, not all conflict is troubling for students. Most peer aggression occurs between students and their friends, and some of this aggression is understood by students to be "just messing around" or jostling. Still, 25% of elementary students reported that they worried about other students being mean to them. Peer aggression is most worrisome for students when it comes from other students who are not their friends and who are stronger and difficult to confront. Problems with social isolation are less common, and only 5% of elementary students replied *never* to the question "I have a friend to play with and sit with at recess." In some cases, all of these problems could be attributed to a fourth, "hidden" problem: Sometimes recess is boring and uneventful, and students argue or fight in a last-ditch attempt to have a little fun!

Of all of these problems, adults in the school worry most about conflict and aggression. One obvious reason is that peer aggression can lead to injuries, and adults are necessarily preoccupied with the physical safety of students at recess. Still, safety is not the only reason that adults work diligently to minimize peer conflicts. Adults find peer aggression to be innately disturbing in its intent to do harm to another child— an intent that violates adult principles emphasizing interpersonal harmony and peace. Consequently, most playground policies and rules (written primarily by adults) emphasize safety and cooperation. As I will demonstrate in Chapter 2, this single-minded pursuit of harmony can blind adults to students' perspective on peer aggression: that it is sometimes worrying, often fun, and an inherent risk that must be confronted while students master social competence in settings outside of adults' ready control.

Recently, policy makers across the United States have questioned the validity of school recess breaks. They argue that recess has no apparent purpose in schools, demands excessive resources in the form of facilities and adult supervision, detracts from students' concentration and academic engagement, and takes time away from the studies that students need to raise their test scores in reading, mathematics, and other academic subjects (Pellegrini, 2005; Pellegrini & Bohn, 2005). Forty percent of schools have shortened or eliminated recess breaks in the face of suggestions that recess is dispensable, dissatisfaction with recess conflicts, and urgent needs to refocus attention on basic academic learning (Clements, 2000; Santa, 2007). Other schools have redesigned recess around structured, adult-supervised play in order to minimize the social disturbances that occur on recess playgrounds. In 2005, between 14% and 18% of elementary students in the United States had 15 or fewer minutes of recess each day (National Center for Education Statistics, 2007).

All of this raises the question "What is the purpose of recess?" Our grandmothers called recess "letting off steam" (Moore, 2006), by which they meant that students accumulate

pent-up energy during their hours of sitting quietly and working diligently, and they have to run off that energy in much
the same way that a boiling tea kettle must vent its steam or
explode. Another purpose is implicit in the present-day understanding that vigorous physical exercise is necessary for good
health—students need recess's hard physical exercise to get
their hearts pumping, raise their stamina, and increase their
health. Child advocates cite the United Nations (1989, 1991)
resolution on students' rights to argue that students have a
human right to play, rest, and relaxation. Still, one of the most
elegant arguments for recess is Pellegrini's (2005) treatise, written during a university sabbatical, in which he clearly documents the importance of recess for students' developmental
competence. Especially for boys, the adherence to rules, leadership skills, and cooperation learned through playing games
on the playground parallel competencies needed for successful adjustment in the classroom (Pellegrini, Kato, Blatchford,
& Baines, 2002). In essence, Pellegrini argued that students
need recess to perform better academically and become more
socially competent.

I, too, believe that recess plays a critical role in students'
developmental competence, and so I will devote Chapter 2 to a
description of students' social competence and their peer interactions, as these shift and change through childhood and into
adolescence. Then, Chapter 3 will examine the interface
between classmates' interactions and the recess environment,
including the physical characteristics of the playground, the
availability of games and play structures, the qualities of adult
supervision, and the ways in which these might promote or
inhibit competent social play. In Chapter 4, I will describe a
data-based problem-solving strategy that can be used to
strengthen the recess environment. The focus of Chapter 5 will
be on playground interventions, including simple modifications in routines and practices that minimize conflict and
maximize dynamic and effective peer interactions, and formal
manualized interventions that have been implemented and
field tested in empirical studies of recess interventions. Because
even minor modifications in recess policies and practices are
difficult to sustain over time, Chapter 6 will describe pragmatic
strategies for evaluating the impact of recess interventions
using data that can convince administrators and colleagues
that the changes are necessary and effective. Examples of my
data-based problem-based strategy in real school playgrounds
will be presented in Chapter 7, followed by recommendations

for other resources and references in Chapter 8. Forms, examples, PowerPoint presentations, and other resources to support the Resilient Playgrounds procedures can be found on the accompanying CD, and in the appendices.

Two

Students' Peer Relationships

The emergence of a rich and authentic understanding of students' social competence is one of the triumphs of developmental research in the twentieth century. This research tradition began in the 1950s, with research on human attachment (Ainsworth, 1989; Ainsworth & Bowlby, 1991; Bowlby, 1969), preschool play (Parten, 1932), and classroom climate (Barclay, 1992). It continued in the 1960s and 1970s with examinations of the behavioral underpinnings of aggression and prosocial behavior and explanations of the mechanisms of social reinforcement and modeling (Bandura, 1977). In the 1980s and 1990s, developmental researchers meticulously examined the phenomena of peer acceptance, peer rejection, peer neglect, social networks, and friendships (Asher & Coie, 1990; Asher, Parker, & Walker, 1996; Dodge, 1983). In the last decade, careful attention has been paid to peer intimidation and bullying (Espelage & Swearer, 2003; Olweus, 1991). Successful interventions to strengthen playground environments will be recess routines and practices that are congruent with these empirical descriptions of students' developing social competence (Pellegrini & Blatchford, 2000). Otherwise, as has been so aptly stated by Dwyer and Osher (2000), some of students' very difficult playground behaviors could be adaptive responses to the unreasonable situations that they have been placed in.

Too often, schools have automatically assumed that students who are unsuccessful in their interpersonal relationships lack social skills. Within that oversimplified theory of change, students who struggle at recess invariably need to be taught new social behaviors. Many years ago, a fourth grader disabused me of that idea when he explained, "Beth, we really like you and we like coming here and we don't mind doing this stuff. But we think you ought to know—we already know this stuff. What we really need is a friend." A comprehensive framework for social competence acknowledges the importance of making and keeping friends, negotiating and compromising to resolve peer conflicts, and confronting peer aggression and intimidation. The complexity of this comprehensive framework has been aptly captured in Waters and Sroufe's (1983) definition of social competence as an ability to respond adaptively to the social environment and to take advantage of social opportunities.

Social competence represents an amalgamation of many different abilities and attitudes: social affiliation, social cognition, social efficacy, social acceptance, interpersonal empathy, and social behaviors or skills. Paramount among these is an interest in social affiliation. Socially competent students care deeply about human interactions, and will set aside other ambitions in order to maintain satisfying relationships. For most students, this preference is a powerful motivator that propels them into social interactions even though they are not sure they will be successful. Social interactions can be intimidating because they frequently require split-second judgments about how to respond to a social event, a task that is difficult for adults and is even more challenging for students whose social competence is still incompletely developed. This challenge can frequently be overcome when students have a menu of optional responses; recognizing that they have many different choices for social behavior makes it more likely that they will settle on an adaptive response (social cognition). The demands of social judgment make it all the more important that students be able to tolerate the aftermath of an occasional social mistake (social efficacy). Students who cannot, and who become mired in social anxiety, will be unable to tolerate social risk taking and are in danger of becoming self-isolating and ultimately disliked by their classmates (social acceptance). Socially competent students are also perceptive: They recognize the fleeting and subtle social cues that mark another person's reaction to their social overtures, and they persistently adjust their social acts in response to these cues (social empathy). They behave in ways that minimize conflicts with their peers and use aggression sparingly and as a last resort when resolving disagreements with friends (social behaviors). Often persistence, as much as skill, determines students' ultimate social success because persistent students engage and reengage the other person until they are successful in the interaction. Still other characteristics of socially competent students enhance their value as friends and play partners: They are spontaneous and playful in their interactions, making them fun to be with. Their loyalty to and affection for peers make them dependable friends. They are able to tolerate differences in preferences and opinions, and so demonstrate their acceptance of friends "the way they really are."

To the degree that playgrounds and other social settings prompt these social assets in students, and accommodate social limitations, they provide contextual settings that maximize students' socially competent interactions. Playground routines and practices can prompt social cognitive understanding, provide social opportunities that are minimally anxiety provoking, accommodate a diverse and interesting array of play activities, facilitate widespread acceptance within the peer community, and directly coach effective social behaviors and prosocial empathy. Ultimately, the impact of resilient playgrounds will be that students who play there will form and maintain satisfying friendships, cope adaptively with incidents of peer aggression and conflict, and defend themselves against instances of bullying and social intimidation.

STUDENTS' FRIENDSHIPS

Students' friendships are dyadic relationships in which each child identifies the other as a friend, they enjoy being with each other, they choose to play or work together when given the choice, and the friendship persists over time (Asher et al., 1996). Having friends gives students many social, academic, and cognitive advantages. Socially, having friends increases students' social standing within a group, reduces their vulnerability to social aggression, and buffers them against minor social stresses (Pellegrini & Blatchford, 2000). Friends help each other, and students are better prepared to weather difficult situations or changes (like moving to a new class or school) when they are accompanied by friends (Hartup, 1996). Academically, friends tutor each other and solve difficult problems together (Chauvet & Blatchford, 1993; Zajac & Hartup, 1997). Cognitively, they extend each other's understanding through their conversations and shared attempts to master new information. Perhaps most importantly, friends are the tether that binds students to schools: The opportunity to make friends and be with friends is the aspect of school that students value most highly (National Research Council and the Institute of Medicine, 2004).

The nature and purpose of students' friendships change as they mature in age and experience. During toddler and preschool years, students tend to have "convenience friend-ships" (Doll, 1996; Pellegrini & Blatchford, 2000). They play with the children who are available to them—sons and daughters of their parents' friends, children in the neighborhood, or students from their day care or preschool group. Within these friendships, a "good" friend is someone who is fun to play with. Indeed, from early infancy, students enjoy interacting with other children and will seek out opportunities to play together. Still, convenience friends are not necessarily "preferred" play partners. Instead, their interactions can shift from one minute to the next as children opt to play the games that are most attractive. Moment-to-moment changes in play partners can leave students isolated when their friend has been attracted away by a more interesting game. Consequently, an important skill in convenience friendships is the ability to approach and join a new group of friends without disrupting their ongoing play. Many kindergarteners and first graders are still playing within convenience friendships.

Sometime in the first or second grade, most students shift into "barter friendships" (Doll, 1996; Pellegrini & Blatchford, 2000). These are dyadic relationships in which each friend favors the other through the exchange of preferred treatment (e.g., "I'll sit next to you at lunch"), favors (e.g., "I'll invite you to my birthday party"), or assistance (e.g., "I'll stand up for you if someone picks on you"). Within barter friendships, a good friend is someone who holds up their end of the bargain: They reciprocate for favors received. Barter friendships serve students' immediate needs by providing them with stable and dependable play partners and frequent and enjoyable interactions. In fact, most early elementary students interact predominantly with a small group of barter friends. Important competencies for maintaining these friendships are the capacity to recognize and track reciprocity in a relationship and a facility for prosocial behavior that helps and supports friends.

By the late elementary or middle school grades, students' friendships transform, once again, into "loyal friendships" (Doll, 1996; Pellegrini & Blatchford, 2000). These are stable friendships that persist over several months or even years in which each friend feels a commitment to help the other socially, emotionally, and personally. Loyal friends find each other because of their easy access to one another (being in the same class or neighborhood) and because of their surface similarities (age, grade, or gender), but also because of their common interests, values, and personal characteristics. Like the barter friendships, these are reciprocal relationships, but the favors that are bartered are often social or psychological: a sympathetic ear in difficult times, reassurance in the face of difficult tasks, assistance with social problem solving, or personal understanding and caring. Conflicts and disagreements will inevitably occur, as they do in all forms of friendships, but loyal friends feel responsible for compromising, negotiating, or even conceding in order to continue their friendship. Loyal friends derive a deep satisfaction from these relationships. Most students are involved in multiple loyal friendships, but they are likely to favor some friends over others and identify best friends, good friends, or casual friends. Essential skills for maintaining loyal friendships include interpersonal perspective taking, facilitating friends' ability to understand each others' point of view and anticipate appropriate ways to support each other; social problem solving, so that friends are able to identify and commit to compromises for minor conflicts and accommodate each others' differences; and conciliation, so that friends are able to balance their own needs with those of their friend.

Students' friendships begin to resemble those of adults by late middle school or early high school, when most students begin to form "intimate friendships" (Pellegrini & Blatchford, 2000). By this time, students are capable of finely tuned perspective taking that makes them sensitive to the emotional and cognitive perspectives of their friends, and they have more extensive repertoires of social behaviors, so that they are better able to respond in skilled ways to their friends' intentions and interests. Their friendships are intimate in the dreams and aspirations that they self-disclose to friends, and the reciprocal interest that they show in more fully understanding the inner selves of their friends. Intimate friendships are also more committed than the earlier forms of friendships. Although friends will still sometimes act in ways that are insensitive or uncaring, intimate friends expect the friendship to persist through these kinds of tensions and trust that they will be able to repair all but the most egregious slights. Intimate friendships require a capacity for trust and authenticity, and the ability to place friends' needs ahead of one's own, at least some of the time.

CLASSMATES

Students are most likely to play at recess with other students from their same class, such that classmates hold a special influence over the friendships and interactions that emerge on a school playground. Not all peers in a class will be friends. Instead, some will be acquaintances, likeable classmates, occasional play partners, or even enemies. The degree to which students are able to negotiate all of these different peer relationships will define their social status within a classroom. Social status has been defined as the degree to which any single student is liked by or preferred by all other students in the class. Four subtypes of social status have been defined within the developmental research: accepted, popular, rejected, and neglected. Accepted students are those who are generally liked by and considered to be acceptable play partners by most other students in the class (Asher & Coie, 1990; Asher et al., 1996). Most of these students will have at least three good friends among their classmates, and will show appropriate social competence for their age and grade. Students who are very strongly preferred by most of their classmates and who hold exceptional influence over social decisions in the class are called popular students. Most popular students are also exceptionally competent socially and have an unusually large number of friends within the class. In some cases, however, popular students are those with very strong social power that makes them social leaders in the class despite an aggressive or thoughtless style of interacting with other students. Some students may be actively disliked by most of their classmates because they either are difficult to interact with or are exceptionally aggressive and mean. These students are called "rejected," or, if they are disliked by some classmates and actively liked by others, they might be called "controversial" students. Finally, some classrooms have students who are neither liked nor disliked; instead, they can be socially invisible students who are often isolated, have only a few friends, and may be forgotten when students are making their plans to play or work together. Researchers call these the "neglected" students.

These social structures can be quite inflexible and can comprise a social "pecking order" within some classrooms. Popular students will have the most social influence within a class, followed by accepted students, and then by rejected students. Students who are neglected may simply be overlooked.

As a collective the classmates can influence each others' mutual interactions by reinforcing or showing approval for some social behaviors, and denigrating or disapproving of others. The reactions of the more influential students in the class will hold more sway over the groups' collective behaviors than those of the less influential students, and some behaviors may be prompted or discouraged simply by the presence or absence of attention. Classmates also serve as each others' models for social behaviors, and the degree to which students copy any one student's behaviors is a rough index of the influence or social status of that student. Students are particularly prone to copy the behavior of classmates who they see as interpersonally warm, rewarding, powerful, and very similar to themselves.

These collective social influences that emerge within a class can be either positive and prosocial or negative and antisocial, depending in part on the students who lead the class and, in part, on the habitual ways of being that have emerged within the class over time. Students can make deliberate efforts to shift or change these group norms, but their efforts can be met with mixed success. Negotiating a shared agreement to reshape social interactions within an entire classroom group is a very advanced social skill that requires finesse, careful reflection, and persistence. When it works, the results can be gratifying. For example, students in one fourth grade classroom reported very low rates of peer conflict on a "recess report" (Doll, Murphy, & Song, 2003). In a subsequent classroom meeting they explained that the fifth graders in their school had an exceptionally difficult and conflict-plagued recess and they decided that they did not want to be that way. Instead, they only played games that all classmates could join, and they made a rule that everyone in the class was welcome to play. In another school, teachers asked a fifth grade boy with exceptionally high social status to befriend Li, a new student in the class who spoke little English and was prone to very intense and difficult temper tantrums. As a result, Li was fully included in his classmates' games, and when his temper began to cycle out of control, his friend was often able to stop it by whispering a few comments in Li's ear. Still, in cases like Li's, adults' efforts to shape the classroom norms have not always been successful. Some students do not have the interpersonal finesse needed to shift their classmates' social habits, whereas others are not committed to doing so. Perceptive adults will work carefully to see that the class's private behavior, outside the sight of the teacher, is consistent with the new norms.

STUDENTS' AGGRESSION

In casual conversations, adults talk frequently and with great concern about students' aggressive actions toward one another. There are stereotypic preconceptions in these conversations that childhood aggression is highly disturbing, clearly antisocial, and evidence of serious emotional disturbance; and that it occurs principally between students and their enemies. As one example of stereotypic thinking, I once asked my sixth grade daughter to help me understand some recess data from a fifth grade class. How was it possible, I asked, for the class to tell me that there were serious problems with arguing and fighting at recess and, at the same time, tell me that they had a lot of fun? The answer was obvious to my daughter: "Fighting is a lot of fun," she carefully explained.

What is aggression? Aggressive acts are actions that students take with the deliberate intention of hurting the other child or forcing the other child to do something (Crick & Gropeter, 1995; Leff, Costigan, & Power, 2004). Although a primary focus of adult attention, observational studies suggest that aggression occurs in fewer than 2% of playground interactions (Blatchford, Baines, & Pellegrini, 2003; Pellegrini, 2005). Leff et al. (2004) reported a considerably higher rate of aggression for an observational study of an urban playground but also described very low rates of interobserver agreement. Results like these illustrate how difficult it is to recognize peer aggression simply by watching students interact.

In most cases, the aggression has one of two purposes: The students have the goal of gaining something from the other child, such as a toy or lunch money or a preferred place in line (instrumental aggression); or the students are seeking to hurt or coerce the other child either in retaliation or as a hostile act (hostile aggression). Property disputes or other instances of instrumental aggression are the most common purpose underlying students' aggression (Humphreys & Smith, 1984). Some of these acts of instrumental aggression may represent a form of justice. For example, when coming in from recess, a second grader left his sobbing friend at the classroom door to chase down and grab his friend's watch back from the fourth grader who had just stolen it. Or, a fifth grader punched a classmate and bloodied his nose in an attempt to stop the classmate's relentless teasing of a kindergartener. Adults struggle to respond to these aggressive acts that clearly violate school rules, but also restored some fairness to a very unfair peer interaction. In most cases, the adults will enforce the rules but with ambivalence. Usually, the avenging students know that their actions will have punitive consequences but believe that the justice is worth the penalty.

Hostile aggression is more troubling. Students may deliberately hurt one another if they are angry because they enjoy the other child's misery or as a payback for a previous injury or insult. It is almost impossible for adults to tell the difference based on observation alone, but adult judgments about the seriousness of the violation will vary depending upon its cause.

Whether instrumental or hostile, students' aggressive acts can be direct physically aggressive behaviors, direct verbally aggressive behaviors, or indirect relationally aggressive behaviors (Crick & Gropeter, 1995). Physical aggression includes pushing, shoving, hitting, kicking, or similar behaviors that physically hurt the other child. Most researchers also include threats to hit, push, or shove as an example of physical aggression. Although physical aggression can occur at any age, it is most common in the early elementary grades and is almost routine in preschool play. By the later elementary grades, most students have been socialized to avoid physical aggression, or to be surreptitious if they do attack another child physically. Verbal aggression includes teasing, insulting, cursing, or name-calling with the intention of embarrassing the other child or "hurting the child's feelings." Adults stereotypically think of verbal aggression as a less damaging form of aggression, and playground sanctions against verbal aggression are not always enforced as vigorously as those prohibiting physical aggression. However, researchers have demonstrated that verbal aggression is highly disturbing for students and has effects that are as destructive and as long-lasting as those of physical aggression. In recent years, a third form of childhood aggression has been discussed: relational aggression. Relational aggression describes acts that students engage in with the intention of disrupting or even ending a child's social relationships with other peers. Examples include exhorting other students to not let a child join their play, deliberately and conspicuously ignoring a child, or saying or doing things to stop other students from befriending the child. Like verbal aggression, relational aggression can be difficult for adults to detect and can be highly disturbing for students to endure.

Indeed, one of the reasons why adults do not always respond effectively to childhood aggression is that they do not always recognize when it is occurring and when it is not. Watch any school playground, and you will see obvious instances in which students hit, shove, trip, or tease each other, or call each other names, and then laugh together afterward. Occasionally a playground monitor will walk up to interrupt the fighting, and the students will look surprised or disgusted, and will protest that they were "just messing around." In fact, students frequently "play fight" with their friends, and when they do, they have no intention of hurting or harming their friend. Instead, this capacity for jostling (also called *rough-and-tumble play*) is one mark of good friendships. In one study of four British elementary schools, jostling was six times as frequent as actual aggression (Blatchford et al., 2003). The most obvious difference between jostling and actual aggression is that both students appear to be enjoying the interaction, and they will remain playing together even while the jostling is ongoing. Careful observation may show that the students are taking turns playing the role of the aggressor or that of the victim. In many cases, though, an outside observer will find it very difficult to tell the difference. The physical or verbal acts are often identical to those of true fighting and arguing, and it is principally the students' *perceptions of* and *intentions for* those acts that are different. In fact, students in Murphy's (2002) classroom meetings reported that they were sometimes unable to tell whether the other child was behaving that way "for fun" or "to be mean"—and the difference was very important to them. Arguments can emerge out of this confusion when students misunderstand their classmates' intentions, but jostling also hones students' skills at managing and understanding aggression (Pellegrini & Smith, 1998).

Alternatively, adult observers may not notice students' aggression even when it is very clearly intended "to be mean" and is particularly hurtful. In part, this is because students are most likely to behave with hostility in unstructured settings like playgrounds, the milling-around time that occurs before and after school, or during the walks to and from school (Leff, Power, Manz, Costigan, & Nabors, 2001). These are times and places when adult supervision is less meticulous, and when students are least likely to be caught in the act. In fact, any astute child could give adults a frank tour of the schoolground and point out the places where aggressive behaviors are most likely to occur (LaRusso, Brown, Jones, & Aber, 2008). Also, many aggressive behaviors can occur almost invisibly—verbal taunts can be said in a soft voice, teasing can occur through looks or gestures when adults' backs are turned, and other students can be pledged to secrecy. Finally, the targets of aggression might "lose face" if they are noticeably disturbed by the aggression, and so they frequently act as if the act was jostling or, at least, unnoticeable. There are a few rules of thumb to help adults discriminate when instances of hurtful aggression have occurred: In most instances, the targets of the aggression will escape or try to flee if they are unable to defend themselves—such that any play that might have been occurring is interrupted by the aggression. Targets of aggression will sometimes be willing to talk about the incident afterward with an adult, if they are outside the notice of the aggressing child.

Bullying is a special case of peer aggression that occurs repeatedly, it is intended to hurt or coerce, and the targets of the aggression are weaker than the bullying students and less able to defend themselves against the aggression. Adults' consciousness about childhood bullying has been raised a lot in the past few decades in the aftermath of tragic childhood injuries or deaths. As of December 2008, 35 state legislatures had passed laws requiring that schools put in place programs to stop bullying from occurring (High, 2008). Estimates of the prevalence of peer bullying differ dramatically, depending upon how bullying is defined and how incidents of bullying are identified or assessed. For example, Leff, Kupersmidt, Patterson, and Power (1999) estimated that between 20% and 30% of students are involved in bullying as victims, bullies, or bully-victims. Batsche and Porter (2006), similarly, estimated that 10% to 20% of students are involved. It is fair to say that almost every elementary and middle school child encounters bullying as a bully, a victim, or an onlooker. In our own research (Doll, Kurien, et al., 2009), approximately 23% of elementary and middle school students report that they worry *often* or *almost always* about other students hurting them on purpose. Unlike jostling, in which both students are having fun, or typical peer aggression between friends in which both students are concerned about and want to end the conflict, bullying is a situation in which some students enjoy perpetrating the aggression, whereas other students (the targets) seek to escape or end it.

The disparity in power that characterizes bullying makes it imperative that adults step in to stop the bullying when it occurs, and institute rules, consequences, routines, and practices that prevent bullying from occurring in the first place. Moreover, because bullying often occurs outside of adults' immediate supervision, effective bully prevention programs work with the peers of bullying and victimized students, preparing them to step in and interrupt bullying when it occurs. Students who are frequent victims can also be taught simple strategies to protect themselves from the aggression. For example, a group of eight frequently victimized second graders listed several "bully tricks" that they could use to protect themselves, including joining or staying with a group of other students, playing near the playground supervisors, blending into the background of the playground by staying busy playing, and never giving older or stronger students an excuse for payback (Swearer & Doll, 2002). Most bully prevention programs are wary of directly confronting bullying students on specific instances of bullying out of concern that they might retaliate against the victim. Instead, researchers in Great Britain have experimented with a no-blame response to bullying that induces empathy for the injured child on the part of the onlookers and the bully (Maines & Robinson, 1998).

STUDENTS' SOCIAL ISOLATION

A less recognized problem is that of students without friends. Indeed, most students have friends, and these friendships provide them with important enjoyment and social support. Friends sit with them at lunch, walk with them to and from school, help them with schoolwork or personal problems, and play with them on the playground. In our own research, 72% of elementary and middle school students say that they *often* or *almost always* have friends that like them as much as they like other people, and these friendships can bind students to school and academic success. Sadly, between 3% and 5% of school-aged students do not have a friend in school, which translates into approximately one student in most classrooms. There is some evidence that the number of students without friends increases as they transition into middle schools (Pellegrini & Bartini, 2000). Students without friends struggle to make their way through daily tasks that other students delight in. For them, walking to school becomes a chore, lunch is a face-saving exercise in pretending to be comfortable and relaxed while sitting on their own, and recess requires that they look like they're having fun and pretend that they play alone from choice and not necessity. As one very isolated third grader explained to me, "I think a lot about Mahatma Gandhi. You know, he talked a lot about nonviolence. I think that most of these kids are too violent for me to want them as friends." A few weeks later, I heard the same child whisper to himself, "I wish, just once, someone would ask me to play."

In some cases, their friendlessness is temporary—new students to a school may take several weeks before making some friends that they can be with. In other cases, however, the students without friends are socially awkward or anxious and are frequently not noticed by classmates, or they are socially inept, much too aggressive, and actively avoided by other students in the school. Sometimes they are strikingly different from most students, in either their appearance or their abilities or behavior. Students who are socially isolated are also much more likely to be the targets of bullying, be unsuccessful in school (and even to drop out of school without graduating), and develop emotional disturbances (Doll, 1996; Pellegrini & Bartini, 2000).

Regardless of the cause, schools should be alert to instances of serious social isolation when these occur, and should interrupt students' cycle into extreme social withdrawal. For example, in a Friendship Group, students themselves were prompted to take control over their social interactions—setting gradually more ambitious goals to initiate play, take social risks, and make new friends (Gettinger, Doll, & Salmon, 1994; also see the Parents' Friendship Meeting Handbook in Appendix H and on the *Resilient Playgrounds* CD). Even very simple social approaches may be unfamiliar to isolated students when they are waiting for other students to reach out to them. One fifth grader who had experienced friendlessness in the fourth grade explained, "When I was new, I thought that the other kids should be coming up to me and making friends, because I was new. Now I understand that they probably didn't notice that I was alone, and that I had to be the one to take the first step." It is also possible to engage all students in a class in fixing the problem. A fourth grade class decided that they would create a welcome program for all new students in their class, appointing ambassadors for new students during their first three weeks in the class, and changing the ambassador every week so that the new students could become friendly with at least three different classmates.

STUDENTS' PLAY

Perhaps one reason that schools have underestimated the importance of recess is that it is mostly about play. Play is easily dismissed as a frivolous pursuit of students that they will set aside once they enter into the adult worlds of work, responsibility, family, and community. Indeed, these stereo-typic assumptions about play are captured in the *Webster's Desk Dictionary* (1983) definition of play as "an exercise or activity for amusement or recreation." Within this frame of understanding, play serves no serious or immediate purpose, is prompted by enjoyment alone, and contributes little to the student, school, or community.

In this book, I take the opposite position, arguing that play is not only purposeful but also essential to the developing child. Within schools, play provides opportunities for respite, recharging weary minds and making it possible for students to resume their studies rested and renewed (Pellegrini, 2005). Physically vigorous play strengthens students' concentration, builds their physical strength and health, and enhances the quality and the persistence of their academic work once they return to the classroom (Pellegrini & Smith, 1998). As a social activity, play provides students with opportunities to practice social actions and binds them to the school so that they look forward to arriving each morning with anticipated enjoyment. Within the broader social community, play makes it possible for students to fine-tune their social competencies and allows them to practice the social roles that they will take on as adults (Pellegrini & Smith).

In describing the emergence of play in the developing child, Parten (1932) described its three stages: solitary play, parallel play, and cooperative play. Solitary play describes students' isolated interactions with enjoyable objects (toys) or their practice of enjoyable activities; it requires little or no inter-personal interaction. In parallel play, two students play along-side one another, and their actions show that they notice and even influence each other's activities, but they do not interact directly. Cooperative play is interactive play, in which students play with one another, and the play actions of one are at least partly in response to the play actions of the other. Although Parten described these as developmental stages in play, cur-rent thinking is that these are also play strategies that all stu-dents engage in at one time or another (Pellegrini & Blatchford, 2000). Importantly, the social cognitive demands for each type of play are very different. Solitary play requires little or no social problem solving and does not require that students use any perspective-taking skills to adjust their play to other peo-ple. Parallel play requires some social judgment, so that stu-dents are able to notice and interpret the intention and impact of the other students' play, and select those activities that are most valuable to imitate or respond to. Cooperative play can be highly demanding socially, and requires that students not only empathize with and perspective take with the other students, but also adjust their actions so that these are most likely to maintain the play over time.

Play within games can be differentiated from freeform play, and the two serve very different purposes (Pellegrini, Blatchford, Kato, & Baines, 2004). When play occurs within games that have preestablished codes of rules and procedures (such as soccer, tetherball, or baseball), it provides students with practice in conforming their social behavior to codified roles. Alternatively, interactions that occur within freeform, made-up-on-the-spot play are typically crafted by the play partners (as occurs while students play store, trucks and highways, or save the king). These kinds of play provide students with practice in negotiation, compromise, and social bartering.

An essential characteristic of play is that it is fun—and having fun together is the foundation upon which friendships are built. Indeed, one of the easiest ways for adults to prompt caring, authentic, and rewarding friendships for students is to create multiple and varied opportunities for students to have fun together. There are many sources for play's enjoyability (Rubin, Fein, & Vendenberg, 1983). During functional play, the activity itself is enjoyable—feeling the breeze on your face as you run, or the wonderful sensation in your stomach as you swing around a merry-go-round. In symbolic play, fun emerges out of students' reenactment of the adult roles and activities that they hope to assume in their futures. Mastery over risk is enjoyable, both in its sense of accomplishment and in the emotional and physical burn that accompanies success.

FAMILIES, GENDER, AND CULTURE

Recess, friendships, aggression, and play all occur within the broader social context of families, cultures, and communities. Developmental research of the 1960s and 1970s prompted various theories about the striking impact of ethnicity and culture on students' play and peer interactions (Bernstein, 1972; Eisenberg & Mussen, 1989; Maccoby, 1998). Indeed, even very similar cultures, like those of the United States and Great Britain, can show important differences in playground routines and practices. For example, Pellegrini and his colleagues (2004) showed that first graders in Minneapolis engaged in games with rules more frequently than those in London. They suggested that these differences could be due to different recess practices in the two countries: The Minneapolis schools had only one recess period, whereas those in London had two or three, and the London recess breaks lasted longer.

As another example, Bernstein's (1972) theory predicted that parents from middle-class and lower-class homes would prepare their children to assume different social roles and to act in very different ways, and that the middle-class parents' teaching would be a better match to successful school behaviors. Subsequent research failed to uncover large or striking class and ethnic differences in social behaviors (Pellegrini & Blatchford, 2000). However, there is some evidence that effective parenting practices can predispose children to be more socially competent. Examples include parents who set firm rules for their children but also provide reasoned explanations for the rules (Baumrind, 1989), or parents who gradually adjust their interactions to their children's emerging social abilities (Ainsworth, 1989). Clearly, these practices occur across economic and ethnic groups, and it is reasonable to expect that cultural differences in social behaviors could become very different as communities become more diverse and integrated.

Another common finding is that, left to their own devices, many students prefer to play within their own ethnic groups (Blatchford, 1996; Boulton & Smith, 1993). Still, in a study of London schools, the rate of cross-ethnic group play increased across the school year (Blatchford et al., 2003). Another observational study, in a school with approximately equal numbers of White and African American students, showed that students were more likely to play in mixed-ethnicity than same-ethnicity groups (Lewis & Phillipsen, 1998). Even more encouraging, students are more likely to play across ethnic boundaries when adults organize games on the playground and when playground supervisors use "active supervision" strategies (Leff et al., 2004).

Even very recent research shows considerable evidence of gender differences in play activities (Blatchford et al., 2003), sizes of play groups (Pellegrini & Smith, 1998), and types of aggression (Crick & Gropeter, 1995). Consistent with stereotypic gender roles, boys tend to play more active games than girls, and to play more games with rules (Maccoby 1998; Pellegrini et al., 2004). Still, Blatchford et al. (2003) suggested that by the end of the school year, girls are much more likely to engage in more vigorous games and the sizes of girls' play groups increase as they spend more time in games with rules. Similarly, and unfortunately, there is emerging evidence that girls' rate of aggression is gradually increasing to match that of boys (Gabarino, 2003). Thus, gender differences in social behaviors also appear to shift with differences in settings, experiences, and generations.

Two important conclusions can be drawn from the developmental research on family, ethnicity, class, and gender. First, children of different genders, ethnicity, social classes, and family traditions are likely to come to school with different understandings of how to play and make friends with their peers. Second, these differences in students' social behaviors are not fixed but can shift and change across a school year and in response to different social contexts. The enduring lesson is that school playgrounds need to foster play environments that accommodate these differences (where appropriate) and simultaneously ensure that playground practices do not prematurely limit or restrict any student's social opportunities.

SUMMARY

Developmentally sensitive efforts to strengthen school playgrounds will support students' opportunities for making and keeping friends, coping with the normal peer conflict that occurs, and successfully confronting peer intimidation and bullying. Peer friendships will vary with age and development but, at all ages, children without friends and those who are unable to maintain friendships over time are particularly at risk. One measure of an effective playground will be its success in pulling these isolated students into the everyday play of their classmates. Conflicts among students are unavoidable, and authentic conflicts may be particularly difficult for adults to differentiate from jostling or rowdy play. On resilient playgrounds, particular attention will be paid to supporting students' efforts to resolve conflicts in addition to providing all students with a cadre of friends with whom they can practice compromise and tolerance. Unlike friendships and conflict resolution, the primary responsibility for confronting peer bullying and intimidation lies with adult supervisors and peer onlookers. On resilient playgrounds, opportunities for bullying will be minimized, whereas peer and adult defenses against bullying will be maximized. Chapter 3 will describe

playground contexts that promote peer friendships and conflict resolution and that minimize peer bullying. Then subsequent chapters will describe how these principles can be
applied to school playgrounds.

Three

School Playground Facilities

My understanding of children's play shifted dramatically one wintry day in Denver, while I watched a lively crowd of elementary students rolling giant snowballs on the playground. This was unusual in Denver. Usually, the snow that fell was too dry to pack well—a soft powdery snow—and it was a rare treat to have a lot of snow that was moist and sticky. Still, it wasn't the packing snow that surprised me. Instead, my surprise came from observing seven students scattered across the playground. These were students from my Friendship Group and I had watched their recess on many other days. All the other times, though, these seven students had struggled to join in the play of their classmates and they usually hung out at the edges of playgroups, pretending to have fun. On this day, instead, they were fully engaged in the rough and tumble of the snowball game, and they were having a great time. The difference, I decided, was the snowball game. Rolling snowballs was more fun when the snowballs were huge, and huge snowballs required a lot of helping hands. All of my Friendship Group students had been actively recruited into one group or another, and that made all the difference for them.

The lesson, of course, was that the places where students play have considerable influence over the social competence that they demonstrate. To some extent, the playgrounds are the arbiters of play and thoughtful refinement of the playground is a logical first step toward enhancing the friendships and managing the conflict that occurs during a school's recess. Playground changes are frequently very simple to make, may be penny-wise alternatives to expensive social curriculum, and could be far more reliable "fixes" than ambitious behavior management plans. In particular, this chapter will discuss three important aspects of playground settings that can change students' play: the physical facilities of the playgrounds, the games that are available for students to enjoy, and the nature of adult supervision that is provided. Each of these features determines, to some extent, the success that students will experience on the playground. (The chapter's information is summarized in a set of three "playground checklists" that are available in Appendices A, B, and C and on the *Resilient Playgrounds* CD.)

PHYSICAL FACILITIES OF PLAYGROUNDS

Important physical features of playgrounds include the location, size, landscaping, and play structures. Their design holds particular importance for the playground's safety, its facilitation of vigorous and attractive play, and the opportunities that it provides for social and psychological development (Moore, 2006). Good playground design can prompt low-risk play for students who are easily intimidated, high-activity raucous play for students who need to run off energy, and intriguing and imaginative play that fosters students' cognitive development and learning. Thoughtful changes to a playground's physical features can usually be made one time (with a single expense for the budget), and can frequently prevent recess problems from occurring in the first place. Still, it is not uncommon for schools to try to save money by working around design limitations in their playground, choosing instead to impose new rules ("Don't play near the culvert") or change recess procedures ("Walk all the way around the parking lot to get to the playground"). For example, a middle school was concerned that students would wander over to the far edge of the playground at lunchtime and talk through the fence with former students who had already dropped out of school. They added a rule to the list, "No talking through the fence." However, because the playground was barren and uninteresting and there was little else to occupy the students' time, the school had to assign a couple of extra supervisors to interrupt the fence talks. In the long run, it would have been cheaper for the school to add more games to the playground (making the lunch recess a lot more interesting) or to add an inner fence to the playground to limit the students' wandering. This is often the case with many workarounds: The rules or procedural "fixes" are inherently less reliable and may ultimately be more expensive.

There are no hard-and-fast rules about playground size and location, and many playgrounds for older schools have been located and sized as an afterthought, once the rest of the building was planned. Still, recent interest in playground design has prompted commonsense guidelines that can be used to assess the adequacy of any single playground's location and size (Marshall, 2006; Moore, 2006; U.S. Consumer Product Safety Commission, 2008).

- The playground ought to have clearly defined boundaries so that every adult and student knows exactly where the playground begins and ends, and understands where the playground rules apply. Where school grounds infringe upon a dense urban community, with its accompanying traffic and pedestrian activities, playgrounds will need to be fenced so that the students can play undisturbed.
- It should be possible for students to move easily from the school onto the playground and back without crossing traffic lanes or access roads. In some cases, schools have erected temporary barriers during the school day to close off traffic lanes or shut down parking lots that run too close to the playground.
- When students are busy playing during a typical school recess, they should be spread out horizontally across the playground. If too many students are crowded into dense clusters, it is a sign that play spaces need to be reassigned so that students' games do not bump into one another and cause unnecessary risks (as when balls from one game accidentally hit nearby students) and disagreements (as when students from one game interrupt the play of other students).
- There should be some places on the playground where physically active students can run, jump, wriggle, and roam—burning up the energy so that they can return to their classrooms refreshed and ready to work.
- Wherever possible, playground structures should be appropriate for students with physical disabilities, including students who use wheelchairs or other assistive devices.
- There should be some places on the playground that are shaded and out of the wind, so that students can play in comfort even on hot, sunny days or on cold and windy days.
- Every space within the playground boundaries should be visible to and within easy calling distance from adult supervisors who are arranged strategically around the space.

- In the best of all worlds, every school playground
  would also have some natural settings that teachers
  can use for science experiments, fostering students'
  naturally inquiring minds.

Safety is a prime consideration in the design of playground
facilities, and for good reason. Between 1990 and 2000, 147
children died on playgrounds in the United States, and in
the year beginning November 1998, 205,850 children visited hospital emergency rooms because of playground injuries (Tinsworth & McDonald, 2001). Approximately half of
the injuries and 30% of the deaths occurred on public playgrounds. Half of the fatalities and many of the injuries were
entanglement injuries that occurred when drawstrings or
other parts of clothing become hooked onto playground structures, causing children to strangle. In fact, the U.S. Consumer
Product Safety Commission (2008) strongly recommended
that drawstrings be removed from children's clothing, coats,
or mittens before they enter the playground. The second most
common cause of death (21%) and a common cause of injury
occurred when children fell from playground structures onto
hard surfaces. The majority of these were attributed to falls
from swings, slides, and climbing structures when children
slipped, tripped, or jumped off on purpose. Other prominent
injuries include *entrapment injuries* (when children's heads
become trapped in small openings of playground structures),
protrusion injuries (when protruding bolts, hooks, or rungs cut
or impale children), and *tripping injuries* (when children trip
and fall over stumps, rocks, or abrupt changes in the ground).
Given these trends, the National Recreation and Park
Association (2008) developed a media campaign to promote
national awareness of the top 12 playground hazards: the
Dirty Dozen. They identify the top hazard as improper playground surfacing materials, followed closely by inadequate
space around play structures; protrusions or openings that
can entrap, entangle, or cut; tripping hazards such as potholes,
stumps, roots, or rocks; and a lack of supervision. The U.S.
Consumer Product Safety Commission (2008) has issued a parallel set of voluntary standards that describe the safe design of
playgrounds and play equipment, including recommendations
for the kinds of surfacing materials that limit injuries when
falls do occur, size limits for openings to prevent children's
heads from being trapped in structures, and descriptions of
the types of protrusions that are dangerous to children.

An important point raised by both the U.S. Consumer Product Safety Commission (2008) and the National Recreation and Park Association (2008) is that playground maintenance is as important for playground safety as the original design. Over time, playground structures can break, leaving gaps or snags; cushioning surfaces can scatter; platform barriers can be tugged loose; holes can erode into the grounds; and trash, including broken glass or rusty pieces of metal, can collect on playgrounds. Periodic playground inspections can mend these and prevent injuries.

Many schools have removed some play structures altogether from the playground rather than adapt these to be consistent with the Consumer Product Safety recommendations. For example, seesaws, merry-go-rounds, and even swings are now missing on many school playgrounds. Still, the prospect of risk-free playgrounds is controversial (Moore, 2006). An essential purpose of play is for students to refine their physical prowess and experiment with physical challenges (Beckwith, 2003). Removing all risk from playgrounds simultaneously limits the opportunities that they provide for students' physical growth and development. A more appropriate standard is to ensure that the playground structures are developmentally appropriate for the students who play there.

In addition to safety, physical features of a playground predispose students to particular kinds of play. Structures that are colorful and attractive draw students onto the playground, inciting a joy that is infectious and that fuels more exciting and delighted play. Equipment that is physically challenging begs students to climb and jump and play vigorously. Other structures lend themselves to imaginative play. For example, a city park in Medora, North Dakota, has a miniature frontier town complete with a stagecoach and locomotive, and it is inevitably filled with laughing children pretending to be early settlers. Playgrounds that are created within natural settings encourage students to explore and find bugs, plants, and other specimens to study on site.

PLAYGROUND GAMES

An often overlooked feature of playground design is the games that are available for students to play. Highly enjoyable games attract students into peer interactions and, for previously unacquainted students, impose a predictable order on their play until they become familiar and comfortable with one another

(Blatchford, 1999). Physically vigorous games prompt students to run, jump, and tumble, building their physical health and endurance and then returning to the classroom refreshed and better able to concentrate (Pellegrini & Smith, 1998). Games with clear rules can provide structures that mediate conflicts and disagreements during play, whereas cooperative games provide students with practice working together toward common goals (Leff et al., 2004; Pellegrini et al., 2004).

As I write this, I can't help but remember my father's stories about the games he used to play around his Montana homestead school—made-up games that were fashioned out of sticks, pebbles, horse troughs, outhouses, and other "found" objects that were lying around on the prairie. Students do not necessarily need *things* to play—but when games are not immediately obvious from the structures arranged across the playground, students do need to have a repertoire of games that they can draw upon to fill their recess time with fun and excitement. In generations past, younger children often learned these games from older brothers and sisters or neighbors, and their knowledge of interesting playground games would cascade down through the age groups. In today's smaller families and safety-conscious communities, children's opportunities for free play occur almost exclusively in age-separated groups, and this limits their access to older children's tacit knowledge about play and games. Increasingly, they depend upon adults to extend their familiarity with many different games.

Consider the following example of a large elementary school in a fairly affluent school district. Standing in the middle of the playground, and scanning slowly around the grounds, an observer could see a set of six cloth swings, a 6 ft. × 6 ft. sandbox filled with sand, a large metal climbing structure with rings to swing from, a pad of asphalt for bouncing balls or skipping rope, a large shade tree with a picnic table underneath it, and a very large open field that butted up against a city park. So, why were fourth and fifth graders having a hard time finding something to play? First, consider the developmental appropriateness of each game. Late elementary-aged students rarely play in sandboxes or on swings. A few of them might climb on the structure, but very reasonable school rules made this a low-risk (and consequently somewhat boring) activity for 10 and 11 year olds. The asphalt had potential—but the budget for playground balls had been left in the hands of the school's physical education teacher, and he was very reluctant to spend the budget on balls that soon found their way onto the school's low-lying roof. There were a few tetherball posts on the asphalt, but no tetherballs. And two foursquare courts had been painted onto the asphalt but were located on a hill and drawn half-size to save space. (School leaders did not realize that it is impossible to play foursquare on a slant.) For all practical purposes, the only age-appropriate game that was available to the fourth and fifth graders was the soccer game that was played out on the open field. Even there, though, arguments were frequent because the sidelines were not marked (and students argued over whether or not a ball had been kicked "out"), and neither were the goals (and students argued over whether or not a goal had been kicked.) Consequently, and totally unintentionally, the limited availability of games had fostered a very conflict-ridden playground for the upper elementary grades. Indeed, several students had lost their recess privileges altogether because they had been sent to the office so frequently for playground misbehavior.

Three things are needed for games to be truly available for students: They must have the facilities and equipment to play the game, they must know how to play the game, and there must be someone to play the game with. In this example, one important change was to replace the tetherballs and to relocate the foursquare courts onto the level asphalt. Both of these are playground games that allow for "automatic" joining: To play either tetherball or foursquare, all students need to do is get in line, wait for their turn to play, and then play the next child in line if they win or move to the end of the line if they lose. Automatic-joining games are particularly valuable for socially timid students who are very reluctant to make the first move toward joining other students' play. One fifth grader explained that he had spent four years playing tetherball because he never had to ask if he could join, and his Friendship Group goal was to find something else that he could play. Socially anxious students also benefit when some of the games on the playground are played in small groups, such as jump rope, hopscotch, racing, and some forms of tag.

A second important change on this elementary playground was to establish a weekly games clinic when a new game would be taught during recess. Several students joined an adult in leading the game clinics—searching through references and the Internet to find promising games, recruiting 6–10 students to join that week's clinic, and keeping track of the games that were most interesting and fun. Adding new games to a playground is a relatively simple proposition: All that is needed is for someone to teach the game to a small group of "starter" students who, if they enjoy it, will teach it to other students, and subsequently the game will spread. In fact, providing occasional adult-led game clinics at recess is a useful way to introduce students to new games and has been associated in the research literature with more cooperative play, less rough physical play, and more interactions across ethnic groups (Leff et al., 2004). By carefully selecting a few students who are slow to make new friends and several others who hold some influence over the group norms, it is possible to shift the play that occurs.

The addition of new games was important on this playground because the existing game—soccer—demands a fair amount of athletic skill, and not all fourth and fifth graders were able to play it. Athletically demanding games can be intimidating for many students because they risk irritating their classmates if they join a game that they can't play with at least moderate skill. This is particularly important at the beginning of the school year, because students gradually increase their participation in athletically demanding games later in the school year as they become more adept at playing (Pellegrini et al., 2004). Just as important, every playground will have some students with physical disabilities, and there will need to be games that fully include those students in the classroom's play. A simple solution is to modify popular games to diminish their physical demands and make them more available to all students. For example, simple chase tag might demand lots of physical speed and agility, but other forms of tag create more cooperative games—partner tag pairs each child with a partner who can share the task of running, octopus tag creates a team of students who are "it," or students tag each other in Frisbee tag by throwing a sponge Frisbee (see www.gameskidsplay.net).

Some students truly require lots of vigorous and physically active play during recess, but physically intense games often raise questions about the safety of the play. For example, dodge ball is usually prohibited on the modern playground because students could be hurt by the rushing ball. (And, when we were fifth graders, we called this game Kill the Guy With the Ball.) Red Rover is rarely played because students can be injured when the other players ram into their clasped hands. In some cases, however, these games can become quite safe if alternative equipment or rules are used. For example, dodge ball might be safe when it is played with a sponge ball instead of a hard rubber ball, and Red Rover can be transformed into a tagging game in which the students who are called out have to only run across and tag a member of the other team without being tagged themselves. These kinds of accommodations can keep the vigor in play without sacrificing the safety.

In this school, the fourth and fifth graders' existing game of soccer was an example of a competitive team game in that it has winners and losers and was played in a large team. Competitive games are advantageous in a number of respects: They often have formal rules and procedures that students can use to govern the game, they can frequently be played in larger groups so that more students can be included in the game, and the competition can contribute to very nice bonding within each team. On this playground, however, the soccer game had become so dysfunctional that these benefits were not easily realized. Thus, a third very important change in the elementary school's recess was to restore predictability to the soccer game. The field's sidelines were marked, and some embedded plates were installed to mark the goal posts. Then, soccer rules were researched on the Internet by the students, and a standard set of rules was adopted by all fourth and fifth grade classrooms. Playground supervisors were included in the planning so that they could understand and respond effectively to soccer disagreements when these occurred.

Not all games on playgrounds must be competitive. An entire discipline has been built around the planning and dissemination of noncompetitive games that students can enjoy without having winners or losers. These are also called "new games," or peaceful playgrounds on which students play only cooperative games (Lefevre, 2002). However, many noncompetitive games are unfamiliar to students and so must be taught to them. Other researchers classify games in other ways. Blatchford (1996) described games with balls, chasing games, jumping and chanting games, seeking games, catching games, racing games, and skipping games. The first three were the most frequently played games, and, by the end of the school year, first graders in Minneapolis and London spent more recess time playing these rule-governed games than they spent playing without rules or just hanging out (Pellegrini et al., 2004).

On the elementary playground in this example, the three strategies of repairing playground structures, teaching new games, and refining the rules of competitive games stretched across several months and significantly increased the number of play options available to the upper-elementary grades. Shifting games on this playground did not solve all of the recess problems, but it did decrease the number of students who were sent to the school office for recess discipline and prompted the school to reinstate recess privileges for several students who had lost them.

PLAYGROUND SUPERVISION

How closely should these games be supervised? A defining feature of playgrounds is that the students' play is less closely supervised than their other activities in the school. Students are given broad authority over who they will play with, what they will play, and how their game will proceed. For example, Pellegrini and Blatchford (2000) advised that adults should not direct students' playgroups because doing so would deprive the students of an important opportunity to exercise their own social judgment and practice essential social skills. School staff have forcefully argued that interfering in students' play smacks of social engineering, and that engineered relationships are an infringement on children's basic human right of free association. In that sense, then, playground supervision is minimalist, and playground supervisors have traditionally confined their attention to ensuring that students' play is non-aggressive and safe.

Given very little guidance in how to appropriately monitor students' play, many recess supervisors have assumed a very passive stance: They tend to stand alone or in small groups, rarely moving too far from a single spot on the playground, interacting occasionally with students who wander near them, calling out to and intervening when they observe students breaking an important recess rule, and allowing the recess to happen around them but not necessarily with them. Students find these passive supervisors to be highly predictable. One second grader explained about the spots on his playground. He pointed out that the best spot to go if you need to "get" another student was behind the pipes because the supervisors usually stood about 10 feet in front of the door and, from where they stood, they couldn't see the other side of the pipes. If that didn't work, he explained, there was another spot around the corner by the third grade classrooms—a 6-foot-deep indention in the building that was formed when a new hallway was added onto the original building. Or, there was also a spot inside the slide, where adults couldn't usually see inside the structure. Similar spots exist on many playgrounds, but many could be eliminated with small refinements in the distributions of supervisors around the grounds.

How many supervisors are enough? In one study of 22 Midwestern playgrounds, Siemers (2006) found an average supervisor-to-student ratio of 5 supervisors for every 100 students, but there was wide variation. Two thirds of the schools reported between 3 and 7 supervisors for every 100 students. In general, the level of aggression and misbehavior on the playground drops with higher levels of supervision and more supervisors per student (Pellegrini & Blatchford, 2000; Siemers, 2006).

What can playground supervisors do when students break the playground rules? In most schools, supervisors confront playground misbehavior with a sequence of gradually more severe consequences. Minor or first offenses earn the student a simple but firm command to stop. For more serious or repeated offenses, students are often sent "to the wall"—a clearly identifiable place on the playground where students are expected to stand quietly for several minutes or the rest of the recess. A pattern of misbehavior will inevitably be reported to the classroom teacher, who may impose additional punitive consequences depending upon the policies of the classroom. In the face of very serious or dangerous behaviors, students will be escorted to the school office and given a visit with an administrator—usually accompanied by a phone call or note home to the parents. An ultimate penalty is that some students lose recess privileges altogether for a period of time or permanently—and frequently these are the students who most need to grow in social competence and friendships. It is important to notice that these consequences are not without cost to the adults in the form of extra supervisor attention and classroom and office disruptions. Even more important, these prototypic ways of supervising recess focus almost exclusively on students' misbehavior— violating a fundamental rule of effective behavior management, "Catch them being good."

Recently, an alternative model for "active supervision" has been recommended that engages playground supervisors in supporting all of the goals of resilient playgrounds: reinforcing rules against playground aggression, confronting bullying, and helping students become more socially competent. In active supervision, a playground supervisor actively seeks out and interacts with students who are behaving appropriately as well as those who are misbehaving, participates occasionally in the play of some students, and comments on the play of others (Leff et al., 2004; Lewis, Colvin, & Sugai, 2000). Increasing the activity of a school's playground supervisors significantly reduces the rate of problem behaviors at recess and can strengthen the frequency and quality of interactions among the students. An essential component of active supervision is that effective playground supervisors facilitate students' attention to each other, and not only on the tasks of the game or play (Pellegrini, 1984). Additional strategies for refining and strengthening playground supervision can be found in Chapter 5. A PowerPoint presentation on playground supervision practices is available on the *Resilient Playgrounds* CD.

SUMMARY

Three features of playground settings provide a foundation for effective peer interactions among the students who play there—a physically safe setting for play with a variety of highly enjoyable and developmentally appropriate games supervised by active adult monitors. When all three of these are present on a school playground, students will spend more of their time interacting and playing together, and less of their time in arguments, fights, or rule-breaking. Consequently, a first step in creating a resilient playground will be to evaluate and strengthen these setting characteristics; the playground checklists included on the *Resilient Playgrounds* CD can support these evaluations.

Next, Chapter 4 describes how systematic problem-solving procedures can be used to identify strategies addressing those recess problems that continue to be evident despite the effective playground setting; and Chapter 5 provides additional information about recess interventions that might be used to foster students' friendships, support their efforts to resolve peer conflicts, and minimize peer bullying and intimidation on the playground.

Four

Data-Based Problem Solving

C hapter 2 summarized current developmental understanding of students' social competence and its expression in students' friendships, peer interactions,
aggression, and play. Three interlocking goals were identified
for resilient playgrounds—that students form and maintain
satisfying friendships, cope effectively with peer aggression,
and are protected from bullying and intimidation. Chapter 3
described important features of playground facilities and
recess practices that contribute to or detract from students'
competent play and peer interactions. Simple playground
checklists included on the *Resilient Playgrounds* CD provide
some guidance in applying Chapter 3's principles to a specific
playground. In this chapter, we will explain how to use data-
based problem-solving procedures to make additional playground modifications, appropriate to the unique conditions of
a single school's recess practices, so that students' peer conflict is minimized, and their dynamic and effective peer interactions are maximized.

Systematic problem-solving procedures have four straight-
forward and logical steps: (a) Describe the problem, (b) list
possible solutions, (c) carefully evaluate the strengths and
weaknesses of each solution, and (d) choose one and try it
out. We have modified this process to include two simple
additions—using reliable and valid data to carry out each
of the steps, and forging partnerships in which adults and
students work together to solve recess problems. All of this
occurs within the theoretical and conceptual understanding
of recess, playgrounds, and students' social competence. With
these additions, the elaborated model is as follows:

1. Collect data describing students' shared perception of
   recess, and use these data to create a graphic portrait of
   the school playground. Include in this portrait information about students' friendships and enjoyment of

play, peer isolation, the frequency and nature of peer aggression, and students' worries about bullying or intimidation.

2. Carefully examine the data-based portrait to identify strengths and problems on the school playground, and if more than one problem is identified, list these in priority order. Which problem is the most important one to address first? Which should be handled next?

3. Convene a classroom meeting including the teacher and all students in a class, and talk together about the data for the first recess problem. Do the students think that the data are accurate? What do they think is causing the problem? And, what do they think could be done about it? The students' answers to the last question generate a list of possible solutions to the problem that adults can supplement with additional suggestions.

4. Evaluate how practical and how effective the listed solutions are likely to be. Given the classroom's current time, money, equipment, and staff (or other resources), could the solution be used? If it is used, how likely is it to fix the problem? Students can also help with this evaluation—their understanding of the plan and the possible solutions may be very different from that of the adults. Given this broad and participatory evaluation, choose a solution (or a combination of these) to try out.

5. Write out a plan that lists the solutions that will be tried, including what will change, who will make the changes, when these will be made, and where they will be made. Include strategies to continue collecting data, so that it will be possible to tell whether or not the plan is working. And finally, include a time when everyone will meet to evaluate the progress.

6. Do it. Carry out the plan with meticulous attention to implementing each step of the plan carefully and completely, and following the plan for long enough that it has an honest chance of working.

7. Meet back together, look at the data, talk about what happened, and decide whether to continue the plan (because it is working well), change the plan (because it is working but not quite well enough), or replace it with a better plan (because it is not working at all).

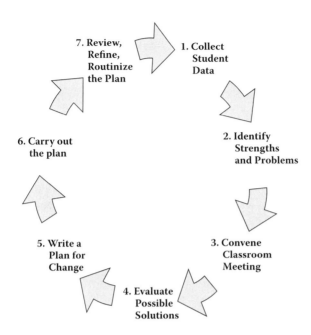

Figure 4.1.   Seven-step Resilient Playgrounds data-based problem-solving cycle.

These seven steps can be used as a cycle in which adults and students work systematically and gradually together to strengthen recess (see Figure 4.1).

The idea of this seven-step problem-solving cycle is quite simple to understand, but putting it into practice can be challenging. In the rest of the chapter, we will describe some practical hints for using each step in the problem-solving cycle to strengthen playgrounds.

STEP 1: COLLECTING DATA

The principle reason for collecting playground data is that, in most cases, adults simply do not know enough about students' experience of recess. Adults' perspectives are shaped by mature ways of understanding, and they have frequently lost the ability to enter into the kids'-eye view of play, games, friends, and fights. For example, a fourth grade teacher thought that her class's excessive bullying was due to a few tough students who had been added to the class. She believed that she needed to be more strict and consistent in restricting recess privileges for these students when they misbehaved. However, other students in her class thought that the bullying was happening because many students were not including their classmates in their play, and that those who were left out of the fun were finding other ways to disrupt the recess. They thought that the class needed to be more welcoming for new students.

A second important reason for collecting recess data is that the data can be a baseline—a starting point against which to measure the success of any changes that are made. Without this baseline, it is very possible that changes in recess practices might be working but so gradually that the progress is not easily detected. Or, perhaps the changes might not be working—but a few good days made it seem as if they are. A data-based baseline provides a yardstick against which to measure change.

The problem with data collection is that, unless it is carefully planned, the data procedures can quickly become too complicated, too time-consuming, and too costly. If this happens, the most common result is that data are collected haphazardly rather than systematically, and the results are too unreliable to use. To guard against this, the playground data must be simple to collect, easy to code into graphs, and accurate in describing what students experience on the playground. In this book, we will use the ClassMaps Survey as an example of a simple and reliable data collection strategy, and in Chapter 6 we also describe other kinds of data that could be used instead with data-based problem solving. (A copy of the ClassMaps Survey is available in Appendix D and on the *Resilient Playgrounds* CD, together with a bibliography of references describing its development and technical properties.)

After experimenting with several different data collection strategies (asking teachers, observing playgrounds, and asking students), we found that anonymous student surveys were a very practical and reliable way to collect playground data, and we developed the ClassMaps Survey (Doll, Kurien, et al., 2009) for this purpose. Although any single student's report of recess could be idiosyncratic and biased, the collective response of all students in the class is quite balanced and perceptive. Collecting student surveys is far more time-efficient than conducting reliable direct observations, and surveys capture students' understanding—a perspective that is often missing when adults attempt to solve problems without data.

To capture this aggregated perspective, items on the ClassMaps Survey were carefully planned to ask the most important questions (with an eye toward the developmental research on social competence and recess practices) that both adults and students were interested in having answered, and using words that are easy for elementary and middle school students to understand. Different classes at different grade levels tried out the survey and suggested changes so that the questions were understandable and useful. Then, statistical measurement analyses were used to evaluate the technical soundness of each item and subscale, and to shorten the subscales so that each was between six and eight items in length. (More information about the technical properties of the ClassMaps Survey can be found in Doll, LeClair, and Kurien, [2009].) Three ClassMaps Survey subscales are immediately useful as playground data: My Classmates (which asks questions about students' friendships), Kids in This Class (which asks questions about peer aggression, including verbal, nonverbal, and relational aggression), and I Worry That (which asks questions about students' worries about peer aggression). (See Appendix D.) Other subscales could also be used to provide supplemental information: My Teacher (which asks questions about the quality of the relationship between the teacher and the students), Following Class Rules (which asks questions about how well students in the class adhere to the classroom rules), and Talking With Parents (which questions whether students talk with their parents about the things that happen at school).

The critical importance of having friends and being a friend was explained in Chapter 2. Using the My Classmates subscale, students can describe the adequacy of these friendships with items like *I have friends to eat lunch with and play with at recess* and *My friends care about me a lot*. High ratings reflect students' collective belief that they have friends who are fun to be with, care about them, and will stick up for them. It is reasonable for ratings to be lower on My Classmates at the beginning of a school year, or if there are a lot of new students who have just joined the class. Otherwise, lower ratings would suggest that students need help finding enjoyable play partners in the class or that they are struggling to maintain friendships over time.

Because peer aggression can occur in many different ways, the items on the Kids in This Class subscale capture students' perceptions of peer aggression that is verbal, physical, or relational. Questions ask students about "kids in this class" and not about the students' own behavior because this wording encourages students to be nonjudgmental and frank in their responses. Because the questions on this subscale are all worded in the negative (*Kids in this class hit or push each other*), all of the items are reverse scored. Higher ratings on this subscale occur when students report relatively less aggression, whereas lower ratings mean that students believe that there is frequent aggression on the playground. On this subscale, it is important to notice when only some items are low because this might mean that only certain kinds of peer aggression are problematic (e.g., *Kids in this class say bad things about each other* or *Kids in this class tease each other and call each other names*). Usually, verbal aggression is occurring more often than physical aggression.

It is difficult to collect accurate survey data about the occurrence of peer bullying, particularly in the elementary grades, because students do not always distinguish between bullying (in which a weaker student is repeatedly victimized by a stronger and more capable student) and just being mean (which might be an isolated event and could occur between students of equal power). Because of this, the ClassMaps Survey assesses bullying and intimidation by asking students how much they worry about being the target of peer aggression. The rationale is that students are much less likely to worry about incidents that they are able to rebuff or that are infrequent, but they will become very anxious about aggression that leaves them feeling helpless and that is likely to happen again. Items on the I Worry That subscale ask students about the many different forms of aggression: verbal, physical, and relational. Because the questions on this subscale are all worded in the negative (*I worry that other kids will hurt me on purpose*), all of the items are reverse scored. Higher ratings on this subscale occur when students report less worry about being hurt or intimidated by peers. Like the Kids in This Class subscale, it can be useful to pay particular attention to the kinds of aggression that students worry about the most, and in most cases, the type of the aggression that is problematic on the I Worry That subscale will be the same type of aggression that is problematic on the Kids in This Class subscale.

So that the survey questions are easy for students to answer, every ClassMaps item has the same response choices: *never, sometimes, often,* and *almost always*. Having four response choices means that if students believe that the answer is somewhere in the middle, they have to choose whether it is toward the negative or positive side of the middle (*sometimes* or *often*). For adult surveys, items often alternate between positively and negatively stated items, so that someone completing the survey cannot just mark every item *almost always*. However, this kind of item reversal can be quite confusing for students, and reliable response sets provide a more defensible and understandable survey design. Instead, simply eliminate surveys in which students made the same response for every item.

Early in our work with classrooms and recess, it was obvious that students' data are most reliable when they are included in the reflection and planning about recess as well as participating in making the data. As one seventh grader explained, "I get it! This is all about trying to fix our school. I think that if you told us that before we answered the questions, I think we'd tell the truth." Consequently, the best practice is to discuss all of the Resilient Playgrounds problem-solving steps with students even before the first survey is handed out. In some classrooms, students have even asked to add a question or two to the surveys, or they have taken responsibility for counting and graphing the answers. To the degree that the students gain a sense of ownership over the process, the data that they generate are more likely to be honest, genuine, and useful.

STEP 2: EXAMINING THE DATA
FOR STRENGTHS AND WEAKNESSES

How do you make sense of the data? The simplest way is to represent the data in a graph so that adults and students can quickly and easily understand the results. For the ClassMaps Survey, trial and error have taught us to use a simple stacked bar graph, where each bar stands for a different question, and a different section of the bar represents the number of students who gave that answer to that question. An example of a ClassMaps bar graph is shown in Figure 4.2. All bars for a single subscale are displayed on a graph, and three graphs represent the ClassMaps Survey responses for all three peer relationships subscales: My Classmates, Kids in This Class, and I Worry That.

To make interpretation even easier, a line could be drawn across the graph. For example, a reasonable decision rule is that data from the My Classmates subscale would be acceptable if the majority of students said *often* or *almost always* to questions describing their classroom friendships. By drawing a line at 60% of the classroom's students, it would be easy to determine whether these two sections of any bar fell below the line. The same rule could be used for the remaining two subscales, although the acceptable responses would be flipped—so

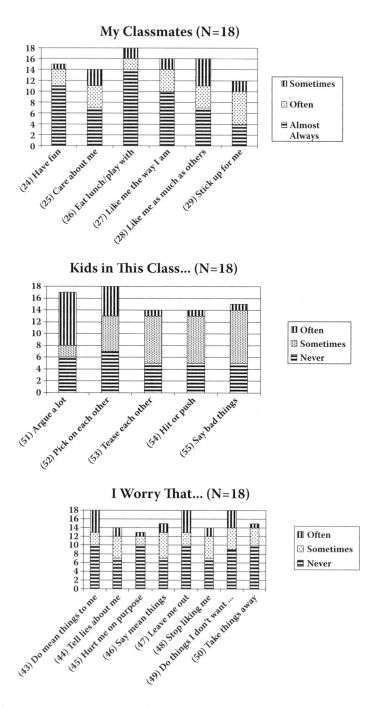

Figure 4.2. Example of a ClassMaps Survey bar graph.

that the majority of students said *sometimes* or *never* to questions describing peer aggression or worries about aggression.

Of course, quirks can appear in any set of data, and adults should use their common sense when deciding what a classroom's data mean. For example, in one fifth grade classroom, several very physical fights had occurred when friends were coming to the aid of each other, and then the fighting between two sets of friends cycled out of control. As a result, the principal and teacher had made a new rule—"No stick-ups"—to stop the students from piggybacking on each others' disagreements. Consequently, it was not surprising that students in this fifth grade generally chose *never* or *sometimes* to the item "I have friends who will stick up for me if someone is picking on me." Data that have been distorted by these kinds of local practices should simply be disregarded.

STEP 3: CONVENING A CLASSROOM MEETING

The idea of sharing classroom data with the classrooms' students originated with a group of very capable middle school teachers. When they saw graphed data from their classrooms, they recognized a teachable moment—an opportunity to reinforce lessons in graphing, mathematical averages, problem solving, and the scientific method using data that the students had created and understood very well. Two other important purposes are served by student participation: They are given a forum for inserting their students' perspectives into the planning for recess improvements, and their ownership of plans for changing their recess is reinforced.

Classroom meetings can be difficult with students who are not accustomed to meeting together to talk through a class-wide decision. Shaping an effective meeting requires, first, that there is a clear purpose for the meeting. Effective student participation requires that they do the following: Think carefully about their own recess experiences, prompted in part by the data that describe their collective experiences with their classmates; participate actively in the discussion by adding new information to the class's understanding of recess and by responding productively to the contributions and ideas of other students; stay flexible and open to new ideas that might be raised in the discussion; and piggyback on each others' good ideas—using each idea as a starting point and building upon it. It is particularly important for each student to add to the class's ideas of possible solutions that might make things better in their recess. The more ideas that are on the list, the more likely it is that the class's list will include a useful and highly successful solution.

After showing the survey data to students, four questions guide the Resilient Playgrounds classroom meetings: Are these data correct? What do you think causes these problems? What could adults do to fix the problem? And what could kids in this class do to fix the problem? Clearly, the last question is the most important one—identifying strategies and changes that students could make that would strengthen the classroom recess is an important first step toward writing a practical and useful plan for change. The second question is also important—understanding students' assumptions about the reasons for the problems might provide critical insight into the problems' origins. However, the first question can also be useful—when students believe that the data are incorrect or distorted, they could simply recollect the surveys. Students' expectations for adults to solve recess problems are frequently impractical or unrealistic, but they often struggle to describe strategies that students can use without first talking about adult practices.

Some classes need more structure for classroom meetings than others. Classes that are not accustomed to meeting together will need ongoing prompts and reminders to keep the work of the group progressing. It can be useful to write the meeting's questions on a chart tablet or the board, set a timer to mark off the time spent on each question, call on students by name when they raise their hand, and prompt reluctant students to participate. Other classes have already participated in frequent classroom meetings and will need less structure. They will only need reminders of the simple rules (No put-downs, Everybody gets a say, Add to any idea on the list, and No evaluation until the list is finished). They will probably be able to maintain their attention even if they are sitting in a group on the floor, and may not need to be called by name before speaking.

STEP 4: EVALUATING OPTIONAL SOLUTIONS

A critical step in the data-based problem solving is systematic evaluation of the possible solutions that the class has listed. Some simple strategies can make this evaluation more efficient and accurate. First, some of the criteria for good solutions are already obvious: They have to be possible to carry out (the resource question), they must be likely to work, and the

classroom's teachers and students need to find them acceptable. Any solution on the list that does not meet these criteria
can be crossed out immediately. As an obvious example, fifth
graders in one urban class wanted to play football at recess,
but the school district's insurance carrier had explicitly prohibited football at elementary and middle schools because of
the liability risk. Other solutions are more difficult to judge
because they may be controlled by other people in the school.
For example, it is not clear whether the playground supervisors would change where students were sent to sit for recess
misbehavior or whether the school budget could be stretched
to purchase a new tetherball and post. Cases like these might
become an exercise in classroom advocacy, with students taking the lead in making a request, backing it up with reasonable
and convincing arguments, and representing their class with
policy makers or administrators.

When students wholeheartedly endorse a plan for change,
it is clear that the plan is highly acceptable to them. They
believe that the change is important to make, very likely
to improve their recess, and worth the effort that it would
require to make the change. They are unlikely to object out
loud when the change is made, unlikely to privately criticize the plan or passively co-opt it, and likely to actively
promote and participate in changes that are made. The
importance of intervention acceptability has been repeatedly demonstrated in behavioral intervention research
(McDougal, Clonan, & Martens, 2000; Truscott, Cosgrove,
Meyers, & Eidel-Barkman, 2000). Any plan for change is
much more likely to succeed when the people most affected
by it (the students, teachers, and playground supervisors)
find the plan to be acceptable. Consequently, evaluations of
each solution on the list should carefully consider whether
adults and students (and, in some cases, the playground
supervisors) understand the change, believe in it, and are
willing to try it.

Once the unlikely solutions have been crossed off the list,
careful attention should be paid to those that are left. The
advantages and disadvantages of each idea should be noted, or
why a solution is especially likely or unlikely to work. In addition, discussion could occur around which ideas are novel and
unlike anything that has been tried in the past. Which ones
are particularly attractive or even enjoyable to the students?
If a new understanding of the cause of a recess problem has

emerged during the meeting, which solutions build on that new understanding to address the problem's cause?

In some cases, the evaluation of the remaining ideas can occur with students as part of the classroom meeting. After a careful discussion of the strengths and weaknesses, students might be asked to put sticker dots next to the ideas that they think are most appealing—with each students having 1–3 dots to vote with. Or, students can vote with hand signals for each idea left on the list—thumbs up for a good idea, thumbs sideways for one that is neither good nor bad, or thumbs down for an unpopular idea. A variation on hand signals allows students to vote with a number of fingers (ranging from 5 to 0) or a number of hands (2, 1, or 0) to indicate their level of support.

In every case, however, the teacher holds the final decision about what solutions to select because teachers hold the legitimate authority for managing problems that occur in the classroom.

STEP 5: CREATING A PLAN FOR CHANGE

Any plan for strengthening recess must describe the specific changes that will be made (the WHAT), WHO will carry out each change, WHEN and WHERE they will carry it out, and a definition of SUCCESS—or simple indicators that can be used as data to track the classroom's progress in improving recess. The easiest way to put the plan into writing is to create a chart with six columns—one for each question. (See Figure 4.3 for an example; a sample planning chart is included in Appendix E and on the *Resilient Playgrounds* CD for your use.) Putting the plan into writing is a simple but highly effective way to make sure that it is actually carried out—it requires careful and deliberate thought about the details of the plan, and ensures that all of the participants have the same understanding of what needs to occur and how.

Data tracking the plan's success is an important part of the plan for change. Figure 4.4 describes a variety of strategies for playground data that are simple to collect, meaningful, and readily available for school classrooms. Only very simple playground observations are listed in Figure 4.4 because direct observations of playground behaviors are among the most difficult measures to collect reliably (Leff et al., 2004). In one study, the notes kept by playground supervisors did not match those of the playground observers (Murphy, Hutchinson, & Bailey, 1983). In another study, the direct observations of

Classroom _____   **Date** _____

WHAT will change?	WHO will do it?	WHEN will it happen?	WHERE will it happen?	What is SUCCESS?	Did it happen?
1.					YES PARTLY NO
2.					YES PARTLY NO
3.					YES PARTLY NO
4.					YES PARTLY NO
5.					YES PARTLY NO

Figure 4.3   An example of a Resilient Playgrounds planning chart.

Measure	Who Completes It?	Why Use It?	How to Use It?	When to Complete It?	And the Data Are:
Teasing thermometer	Students	To measure an amount of something	Mark an X on the thermometer to show how much teasing happened today.	Right after coming in from recess	Class average or sum
One-question check-in (paper and pencil)	Students	To answer simple yes or no questions	Circle the answer to the question: Did you argue today?	Right after coming in from recess	The number of students giving each answer
One-question check-in (vote in a jar)	Students	To answer simple yes or no questions	Put your ping pong ball in the yes, sometimes, or no jar to answer the question: Did you have fun at recess today?	Right after coming in from recess	The number of balls in each jar
Playground tokens (sticky tape tokens, wide rubber band bracelets)	Students	To count the number of times that students have been "caught being good"	Playground supervisors give students a bracelet (wide, colorful rubber band) to slip around their wrist for good recess behavior.	Students slip the rubber bands into a jar or sticky tape onto a chart upon coming in from the playground	The number of tokens in the jar or on the chart

Simple playground observations	Playground supervisors or an independent observer	To answer simple questions about a small select group of students	List 6–8 students with a question: Who played with peers today? Or who was not physically aggressive today?	Immediately after students come in from recess	The number of students who succeeded on a day
Supervisor reports	Playground supervisors	To capture supervisor impressions	Playground supervisors answer a 2–3-question survey about how recess has gone that day.	Immediately upon completing recess supervision	Average or total across supervisors
Playground problem report	Students who are called out for problem behavior on the playground	As a record of problems that occur	Students complete a brief 4–5-question report describing what occurred, with whom, where, what happened, and what they will do differently next time.	Immediately upon students being called out	Number of playground problem reports per day, per class, or per student
Office discipline referral	School office staff, with students	As a record of problems that occur	Students sent to the office for playground discipline are entered into the log.	As students enter the office	Number of office discipline reports per day, per class, or per student

Figures 4.4 Examples of simple playground measures.

relatively infrequent behaviors—physical, relational, or verbal aggression—demonstrated very poor interrater agreement
among independent observers. This is not surprising, given
the research that has already been described in Chapters 2 and
3. Many of the most problematic playground behaviors occur
very occasionally, fleetingly, and surreptitiously—because
students make very deliberate and skilled attempts to con-
ceal their aggression toward one another. However, very sat-
isfactory measures of playground behaviors can be gathered
through global observations of a few students—how many of
the eight most isolated students played with friends today?
How many of the seven most disruptive students played today
without being sent to the wall even once? Alternatively, token
systems can be used to count the number of times that students were caught in positive behaviors. To be practical, the
playground tokens need to be things that can be stuck to students' clothing or placed on their wrist, so that students never
need to hang onto a token while they play. (Obviously, tokens
should not be entrapment hazards, and should be difficult to
counterfeit so the system stays honest.) Such tokens are easy to
collect if students drop them in a collection box or stick them
on a chart as they reenter the classroom.

Often, the simplest data to collect are those that are already
collected in the school for other purposes. For example, one
elementary school had already implemented a schoolwide
behavior management program, and students were given
"strikes" and required to write a note home for rule violations.
In this case, a tally of the number of recess strikes that were
given was simple to collect. In another middle school, students
who were sent to the office at lunchtime were required to log
into the notebook before taking their seat, and the log was a
simple record of the number of office referrals. Students in a
third school were "blacklisted" after three recess violations
in a month, and lost their recess privileges. The supervisors'
violations record was a simple source of recess data.

In some cases, teachers and students will sign the plan.
Signing the plan is a symbolic indicator that everyone is on
board with the plan and agrees to carry it out. Still, even if
the plan is not signed, it should be highly visible. Copies of
the plan might be posted next to the classroom door, where
students will see it as they leave the classroom for recess. Or,
an abbreviated description of the plan might be included in a
classroom's newsletter that they send home to parents. Useful
strategies are to add a checklist onto the written plan so that

the class can keep a record showing that the planned changes actually did occur, to assign a pair of student helpers to collect the daily recess data, and to set aside a few moments each week to talk about the classroom's plan and how well it is being carried out.

STEP 6: TRYING OUT THE PLAN

Regardless of how simple a plan is, it represents a change from the way things used to occur, and making changes can be difficult. It is always easiest to simply continue doing what has always been done (habitual behavior)—that doesn't require that the class stop and remember the changed procedure, or practice unfamiliar actions. Once a plan has begun to be implemented, it is easy to second-guess it and tempting to make minor modifications. One fix on Monday, a few more on Tuesday, and pretty quickly, the written plan for change bears very little resemblance to what actually occurs on the recess playground. It is far more effective, once the plan has been thoughtfully developed and written down, to follow it for at least two weeks while also building in regular reviews (perhaps every Friday afternoon) to look at the data and talk together about how well the plan is working. Again, students in a classroom can be responsible for important tasks of the plan for change. For example, students can be monitors to check off each plan step from the checklist, and to remind participants of the change.

Where the new activities are difficult or confusing, it is very useful to practice them in a situation where it doesn't really count. For example:

> Let's pretend that we are trying out our new way of choosing teams. If we were going to do this today, Mikalah and Reman would be the team leaders. Why don't you both come up to the front and pretend that you are choosing teams for real? Mikalah, you go first. Who would be your first pick? Alyssa—since Mikalah chose you, you should go and stand on her side of the room. Reman, you're next . . ."

and so on.

Then students might be asked, "What did you like about this? What do you wish we did differently?" Simple procedures can be fine-tuned and meticulously planned, so that they are easy to carry out the first time.

Occasionally, it will be obvious that something that was planned has not really been occurring. For example, a fourth grade classroom made up a "teasing form" for two students to use when teasing occurred on the playground. (See a more detailed description of this example in Chapter 7.) The student being teased and the student who did the teasing would each answer half of the form, and, together, they would develop a list of things that they could do differently the next time. The class practiced using the teasing form (a simplified conflict mediation strategy) during class time, and then copies of the form were placed in a cubby next to the students' other worksheets and materials. Two weeks later, not a single teasing form had been completed—but the teasing had dropped dramatically in the class. What happened? It is possible that another part of the class's teasing plan—saying "Ouch" in a loud voice when someone says something mean—was sufficient to fix the problem. Or perhaps having the form available was sufficient instruction in mediation and the students were able to resolve their teasing incidents. It is possible that completing a worksheet was "punishing" for the students and they avoided teasing so that they would not have to complete one.

STEP 7: EVALUATING AND REFINING THE PLAN

The seventh step in the cycle is a lynchpin step: The plan is working, and it can be integrated into the routine practices of the class; it is partly working and can be refined or strengthened and then continued for another trial; or the plan is not working, and the teacher and students will return to the beginning of the cycle (Step 1) to replace it with a better plan. This decision emphasizes the importance of the data that the class has been collecting all along as part of the plan for change (Step 5). A careful examination of the data should show whether the class has met or approached the definition of success that was written into Step 5's plan for change.

There are many different reasons why plans for change might not work. First, some plans were never really carried out according to the written plan. Perhaps it was too ambitious—as when a class planned to add a new game to the recess playground each week, but no one really had the time to find the games and teach them to the group. Sometimes, a plan that sounded fun was pretty uninteresting when it was actually carried out—as when a class decided to complete a social skills lesson on preventing bullying but found out that the curriculum was boring when they tried it. In some cases, people simply forgot to carry out their part of the plan, and needed more reminders. When a plan was not carried out, it might be sufficient to simply try again and try harder, but it might instead be a sign that the plan needs to be changed to make it more acceptable or easier to carry out.

Sometimes plans do not work because they were not used long enough. In this case, the data would probably show that recess was improving, even though the class had not yet met their goal for success. Plans that are working slowly sometimes need a stronger dosage—making more of the change or making it more often. For example, an eighth grade class found that the number of arguments at their lunch recess had dropped once they took some new games out on the playground with them—but they hadn't dropped far enough. One option might be to add even more games. A fifth grade class found that they wasted less time arguing about the soccer rules once they wrote a soccer rule book, but they still wasted too much time. One option might be to include more peers in the plan by extending it to other classrooms.

Sometimes plans do not work because they were the wrong solution. Perhaps the students and teacher have gained some new insights into the problems at recess, and the changes that might improve it, while they were working with the first plan. In this case, another Step 4 classroom meeting could pose some additional strategies for change that could be more effective.

Finally, some plans do not work because the recess problems have simply grown too strong and difficult to be managed by modest changes in classroom routines and practices. When this occurs, it is time to select an evidence-based manualized intervention that is appropriate for the problem and for the classroom. (Chapter 5 describes the most prominent evidence-based interventions.) Evidence-based interventions will not necessarily be used instead of the Resilient Playgrounds procedures—rather, they can be integrated into the data-based problem-solving cycle. These become the "written plan" for intervention, even while data continue to be collected to describe the success of the plan.

The advantage of evidence-based interventions is that they have been developed by researchers and practitioners who have special expertise in the problem that they address, and there are data demonstrating that these interventions have been effective in other schools and classrooms. The intervention materials and resources are already developed and refined. The interventions that are mentioned in Chapter 5 are those that show the most promise for impact in actual classrooms. Disadvantages of evidence-based interventions are that they often require resources that are not readily available in a school—funds to purchase the intervention, time to carry it out, or expertise or training to use it well. In some cases, the evidence supporting an intervention's effectiveness may have been gathered in a school or community very different from your school—with a different community culture, different family income level, or different school practice. Within the Resilient Playgrounds cycle, decisions to spend school resources on an ambitious evidence-based program will be made knowledgeably when data exist showing that the problem is present, has not responded to less ambitious interventions, and is important enough to change.

SUMMARY

A simple seven-step problem-solving procedure can be used to systematically address problems with students' friendships or peer conflict: Collect data describing students' perceptions of recess, examine the data to identify recess strengths and problems, discuss the data and the problems with students in a classroom meeting, select the best solutions for recess change from students' ideas as well as the teacher's or other adults' ideas, create a plan for change out of these solutions, try out the plan, and revise or refine the plan as necessary. This chapter has explained how to apply these steps using streamlined measures to collect data and ample student participation to strengthen their responsibility for recess improvements.

One of the most daunting steps of this problem solving is identifying and selecting strategies that are likely to fix recess problems, strengthen students' friendships, and minimize their peer conflict. Consequently, Chapter 5 will describe several alternative options for recess intervention that have been used with success by others. Inevitably, this data-based problem solving occurs within a larger context of a community, school district, and school. Ambitious plans for change will need the full support and endorsement of school and community leaders if they are to proceed unimpeded toward success. Chapter 6 describes the kinds of data-based advocacy that can be used to secure this support.

Five

Playground Interventions

KATHERINE BREHM AND BETH DOLL

C hapter 4 describes the use of systematic problem-solving steps to develop and implement classroom plans for improving recess. Of these, Step 3 involves teachers and students in identifying and critically evaluating strategies for solving recess problems—strategies that help students make and keep more friends, resolve the inevitable conflicts that occur between students and their peers, and successfully confront bullying and intimidation from their peers. Chapter 4 emphasizes students' perceptions of the recess problems, and student ideas for making recess more enjoyable. Still, it is also important that adults leading Resilient Playgrounds projects be familiar with a variety of informal strategies and formal interventions to improve playgrounds and recess. This chapter will provide a more detailed explanation of the kinds of strategies and interventions that have been used in other schools to foster resilient playgrounds.

Three kinds of strategies are useful for enhancing school recess breaks: setting modifications that alter the physical features of the playground, changes in recess routines and practices, and manualized intervention programs to develop students' social competence and minimize peer aggression and conflict. Of these, playground modifications are the easiest interventions to implement—playground facilities can be monitored and repaired following a routine maintenance schedule to eliminate hazards and hidden "spots" that are difficult to supervise, threaten students' safety, or disrupt their play. Very clear guidelines for reviewing and repairing playgrounds can be found in the U.S. Consumer Product Safety Commission's (2008) *Public Playground Safety Handbook* and have been summarized in Chapter 3, so these will not be discussed further in this chapter.

Changes in playground routines and practices are the next easiest interventions. Often these are simple additions to or revisions of playground practices that have been suggested by teachers or other adults who are experienced in playground supervision, or have been proposed by the students themselves. Sometimes, they are found in playground research, where investigators have examined the impact of specific playground practices on students' social competence and social behavior. Typically, these changes are embedded in students' or teachers' understandings of the causes underlying problems on a particular school's playground. Even though these altered recess practices have not always been proven effective in systematic playground research, Resilient Playgrounds procedures ensure that there are local data demonstrating their impact. Because monitoring data continue to be collected even while recess changes are made, it will be apparent whether modified routines are strengthening student friendships and reducing peer conflict and aggression. If so, the recess changes can be "routinized" or permanently embedded into the recess practices in order to maintain the success (Doll et al., 2004). If there are no improvements, or if there are insufficient improvements, it may be necessary to revise the plan so that it is stronger, implemented for a longer period of time, or discontinued and replaced with a comprehensive, manualized intervention.

The implementation of comprehensive manualized interventions is the most demanding recess improvement strategy. These are typically multicomponent treatment programs that are guided by a manual that provides precise instructions for activities that should occur with students, teachers, or families, and that are frequently accompanied by prescribed procedures for evaluating the impact of the intervention. They have been empirically tested in carefully designed research studies to verify that the interventions prompt positive changes in students' peer interactions, that these changes are greater than would occur by chance alone, and that the changes are large enough to represent meaningful improvements in social competence.

Given the expense and resources demanded by many comprehensive manualized interventions, it may not be practical to use these for every recess problem that is identified. However, when the classroom's data suggest that an important recess problem is not responding to simple changes in recess routines and practices, a manualized intervention may be necessary.

CHANGES IN RECESS ROUTINES AND PRACTICES

A key advantage of simple changes in recess routines is that these can be fully "localized," or individualized to fit with the distinct playground practices or problems that already exist in a school. This chapter will describe some common changes that have been detailed in playground research. Many other changes have also been proposed by students or teachers who are working together to "fix" their own recess. Table 5.1 provides some simple examples of teachers' and students' proposed changes that were used to strengthen recess practices in their class. There is nothing magical about these particular changes; instead, their power lies in listening carefully to the

Table 5.1. Changes in Recess Routines and Practices

To Help Students Make and Keep Friends

Add at least one "anyone can play" game to the playground.

Teach students to play games that are more fun with more people.

Run a weekly "game clinic" to teach new games, and be sure the students without friends are in the clinic.

Assign pairs of students to complete tasks outside of the playground.

Appoint ambassadors to introduce new students into the playground.

To Minimize Peer Conflict

Shorten the length of the recess.

Make sure there are lots of other ways for students to have fun—add more games to the playground.

Rearrange the supervisors on the playground so that there is more consistent coverage.

Solve the predictable arguments in advance with classroom meetings—write a classwide rulebook for soccer or kickball.

Choose the week's soccer teams on Monday following "pick fair" rules that the class has set.

Students who argue or fight complete a "conflict worksheet" that leads them through the mediation steps.

To Stop Bullying

Find and fix the spots on the playground where bullying often happens.

Make sure that supervisors respond whenever bullying occurs.

Write a weekly "Dear Emma" column where students can get advice for handling bullying, and post the letters and answers on a hallway bulletin board.

Convene a class meeting on "how we want our class to be."

wisdom of teachers and students and carefully attending to these ideas as potential strategies for change.

Routines and Practices That Promote Social Competence

A first important goal for improving recess is to promote students' social competence by maximizing their opportunities to make and keep friends. The mechanism underlying friendships is simple to understand: Friends are made when two students spend time having fun together. Given that, it is easy to see why strategies that enhance the types and organization of games played on playgrounds, and provide occasional adult leadership of games, strongly influence students' playground behavior and enjoyment. For example, Bay-Hinitz, Peterson, and Quilitch (1994) demonstrated that very young children increased their prosocial behavior when led by their teachers in cooperative games and increased their aggressive behavior when led in competitive games. These results were still evident the following day during free play. Similarly with older students, adult-facilitated noncompetitive games such as ultimate Frisbee, obstacle courses, and parachute games provide opportunities for students to practice cooperation and teamwork, learn conflict resolution skills, and grow in confidence and self-esteem (Butcher, 1999). The games also reduce aggressive, inappropriate playground behaviors.

In a related study, Leff and colleagues (2004) divided an elementary school playground into five areas with age- and gender-appropriate structured games such as hot potato, relay races, jump ropes, and hopscotch. They allowed students to move freely among the areas. Each area was actively supervised by an adult who facilitated the games, praised appropriate behavior, and walked around commenting on the students' play. The addition of organized games to the playground resulted in higher rates of cooperative play, lower rates of rough-and-tumble play, and more frequent interactions among students of different ethnic backgrounds. Adult supervision was more effective when supervisors actively facilitated the organized games than when they passively monitored play in the absence of organized games.

Similar strategies have been used during the often unstructured (and undersupervised) time before school, which can be chaotic and potentially dangerous for students who arrive early. The before-school time is complicated because students who arrive early may not know each other well enough to play freely without getting into trouble, and likely represent a broader age and interest range than typically seen on the recess playground. Murphy et al. (1983) investigated whether providing organized games (relay races, jump ropes) and a time-out procedure for early elementary students would reduce the arguments, property abuse, and rule breaking that had characterized the students' before-school behavior. They set up simple starting and stopping points and lanes for races using ropes strung through plastic pipes that had been stuck vertically into the ground. Adult supervisors provided instruction in how to line up and turn the rope for jump ropes. Supervisors were also given a handout listing types of inappropriate behaviors, how to patrol the playground area assigned to them, and how to deliver praise for appropriate behavior and time-out on a nearby bench for resistant students. The intervention resulted in a clear decrease in the most serious types of aggressive behaviors. An unanticipated outcome was that some difficult-to-supervise students who had previously simply wandered around became "fans" who watched the races and cheered for the runners. Thus, these former nonparticipants could now "participate."

Students can also be playground game leaders. Calo and Ingram (1994) taught fourth graders to lead activity stations for the other students in the school during lunch recess. Playground leaders were selected based on teacher nomination, attended training sessions to learn conflict resolution and how to play the various games, and rotated with a partner through several different stations. Then they rotated off the leader team to give other students a chance to develop their leadership skills.

In another study, Chuoke and Eyman (1997) marked off one area of the playground with cones and called it the Play Fair area. It became an inclusive play area where all students were able to join the play of noncompetitive games. Fourth through sixth grade students with varying social styles and skills (including passive, assertive, and aggressive students) were formed into five Play Fair squads of five to six students each. The Play Fair students attended a one-day training in noncompetitive games and communication skills. Every day during recess, a different Play Fair squad selected and led the noncompetitive games for that recess period. No one was required to participate in the Play Fair area, but Play Fair squad members could invite isolated students to join them. Problems and conflicts were referred to adult supervisors on duty. Problem behavior decreased significantly among students in grades four to six both on the playground and in the classroom. A majority of students participated regularly, and students who were once bullies worked actively to make sure everyone was included.

Not every child is eager to try new games or comfortable joining play groups. Sometimes routines and procedures are needed to promote inclusion and prompt students to actively participate in playground interactions. For example, Schoen and Bullard (2002) taught the rules and procedures for a variety of group games to first and second graders, and held discussions about fair play and good sportsmanship. Then a chart was created with the name of each child and the new playground games, and students were awarded stickers each day for playing the games.

Some isolated students are so socially anxious that they need to enter into playground groups very gradually. It is not uncommon, for example, for socially anxious students to hide in the restroom or coat closet rather than go out to recess with the rest of their class, or to routinely not finish their seatwork so that they are required to stay in and work through recess. Playgrounds that are carefully supervised will feel safer to these students, and games that can be played in very small groups will help them feel more comfortable. Still, it is sometimes necessary to also set up gradual "stair steps" in which the bottom step describes what the student is currently doing during recess (e.g., hiding in the bathroom) and the top step describes what the student wants to be doing (e.g., playing outside with friends and having fun). The most useful staircases are between seven and 10 steps high. Then, students can move toward their recess goal one step at a time, setting their own goal for the following day's recess, and earning a small prize or privilege for meeting their goal. Ultimately, staircase programs in which the students design the steps and control the goals will teach students coping strategies for dealing with everyday anxieties. Sometimes, school-based strategies are insufficient to prompt isolated students to make more friends. In this case, parents can be effective "consultants" for their

children who are tackling friendship problems (Gettinger et al., 1994). A manual for a Parents' Friendship Meeting can be found in Appendix H and on the *Resilient Playgrounds* CD.

Routines and Practices That Discourage
Rule Breaking and Peer Aggression

A second critically important recess goal is to increase students' compliance with playground rules and to minimize the student-on-student aggression that occurs during recess. Any routine that provides students with more highly enjoyable games at recess will also discourage peer aggression because, to some extent, fighting and arguing happen when students are bored and have nothing better to do. Second, changes in playground practices that minimize nagging irritations on playgrounds can frequently remove some of the reasons for fighting and arguing. These might include changes to ensure that students' games are spread out and do not bump into other students' play space, there are fair and reasonable routines for students to choose teams, students have a common understanding of the rules for their favorite games, and there are adequate balls, jump ropes, and other playground materials for students to use. Students frequently identify these or similar irritations in their classroom meetings, and, once they do, strategies to eliminate the irritation are often obvious.

Another logical step toward increasing rule compliance is to ensure that students fully understand the rules that govern use of their playground. In one school, playground behavior expectations, safety guidelines, and routines for equipment use and game play were taught in recess workshops that addressed both outdoor and indoor play (Todd, Haugen, Anderson, & Spriggs, 2002). Students received a map of the playground with its boundaries, game areas, and play equipment labeled. Then, for 45 minutes, they walked the playground with their teacher and playground supervisor, trying out the games and equipment and watching demonstrations of how to solve problems. The 30-minute indoor recess workshop focused on classroom routines for free play. As a result, students began to play more cooperatively and office referrals for playground problems decreased.

As has been made apparent in Chapter 3, high-quality supervision is essential for effective school playgrounds. Although it is not common practice, playground supervisors can be systematically trained to carefully monitor and respond effectively to students' recess behaviors. Essential components for this training include the following:

- List and explain the playground rules, including safety rules, rules prohibiting rule breaking and aggression, and rules promoting appropriate playground behaviors.
- Carefully describe (preferably on playground maps) where supervisors should locate themselves.
- Describe how supervisors should move around within their assigned locations and routinely scan the playground for rule violations or problems.
- Explain, model, and act out strategies that the supervisors should use to praise or reward students for positive playground behaviors.
- Explain, model, and act out simple commands that supervisors should use to interrupt minor transgressions.
- Explain, model, and act out the time-out procedure that is used on the playground when students repeatedly violate a rule or ignore a supervisor's command.
- Explain, model, and act out the procedure that will be followed when a student must be sent off the playground when on-playground management strategies are not effective.

A PowerPoint presentation describing effective playground supervision practices can be found on the *Resilient Playgrounds* CD. Ideally, the most important details of the training should be summarized on a 4" × 6" card that the supervisors can carry in a pocket while they are working, and the complete training should be captured with a videotape and training handouts that can be used to repeat training as needed if new supervisors join the playground midyear. Playground supervisors' training will be most effective if they are included in some of the decisions about how the playground assignments are organized or how certain behavior management strategies are carried out. Still, the procedures or assignments may not be modifiable if a supervisor joins a playground assignment midyear or if the school has already codified its playground supervision procedures. Even then, playground supervisors will benefit from simple rationales explaining why these procedures are used and from periodic check-in meetings to make sure that the supervisory routines are still working effectively.

An efficient way to manage peer aggression and rule breaking is to build on existing schoolwide positive behavior support programs. For example, Lewis, Sugai, and Colvin (1998) took overall school rules and developed social skill lessons to teach replacement behaviors for the problem behaviors that were occurring in specific settings, including the playground. First through fifth grade teachers taught the skills using demonstrations and role plays. On the playground, adult supervisors used a group contingency consisting of elastic loops given to students, along with verbal praise and feedback for following the rules. Students placed the loops on their wrists, then deposited them into a jar in their classroom at the end of recess. When the jar was full, the class voted on a group reinforcer. The intervention resulted in a modest reduction in overall level of problem behavior, with positive changes maintained over the following 3 months. In a similar study, adding a precorrection procedure (a brief review of school rules and playground behavior expectations before students went out for recess) and active supervision also effectively reduced problem behaviors (Lewis et al., 2000).

Sometimes, however, reinforcing playground rules and contingencies isn't enough. In an intervention that also built upon a schoolwide positive behavior support program, Lewis, Powers, Kelk, and Newcomer (2002) developed rules and routines for specific activities and games, such as tetherball and soccer, and teachers practiced them with their students on the playground during nonrecess periods. Combined with a group contingency using elastic loops given by playground monitors, this intervention reduced problem behavior on the playground. Although elastic loops are convenient and fun ways to dispense reinforcement, supervisors can also tape "good job" tickets to students' clothing, for later transfer to a book that tracks individual students' reinforcement records (Roderick, Pitchford, & Miller, 1997). The important things are that students do not need an entirely problem-free recess to earn a ticket or an elastic loop, and that more than one can be earned but none are taken away for subsequent problem behavior.

Routines That Prevent Bullying

In many respects, routines and practices to prevent peer bullying are extensions of the strategies that have been used to discourage aggression and rule breaking. Also, routines that reduce overall peer aggression typically also reduce peer bullying. However, some additional strategies are particularly important to address bullying. Most effective bullying prevention programs carefully train all adults in the school to recognize bullying and to interrupt it immediately when it occurs. A primary purpose of this training is to confront pervasive myths about bullying that are so dominant within many communities: that bullying is just an example of kids being kids (when, instead, bullying is a very toxic form of student peer aggression and needs to be stopped) or that students who are bullied just need to toughen up if they're going to survive in this world (when, instead, victims of bullying are almost always selected because they are weaker and less able to defend themselves). All adults in the school need to become vigilant about noticing bullying and intervening to stop it.

A second very important activity for preventing bullying is to sensitize all students in the school to the hurtfulness of bullying, their responsibility for avoiding bullying, and the need to report bullying immediately. Commercial films examining children's friendships are often an effective strategy for opening these conversations with a class. For example, the film *Stand by Me* includes some remarkable scenes describing the very close friendships of four preadolescent boys as they embark on a 2-day journey along the railroad tracks. *Little Man Tate* includes some very compelling scenes where the very gifted and isolated Fred Tate is shunned or made fun of by his classmates. The young adult novel and recently released film *Bridge Over Terabithia* includes some very realistic scenes describing a friendship between a middle school girl and boy, and other scenes depicting playground bullying. A word of caution: The most authentic films describing children's friendships almost always include language or behaviors that violate school rules, so it is important to select video clips carefully so that they omit any prohibited scenes. In some classrooms, teachers have instead chosen chapter books that provide rich friendship themes, read one chapter of these each day after lunch or recess, and build the class discussions around the book. Six questions are useful for shaping classroom meetings or discussions around the bullying problem: Whose job is it to fix this problem? Is it [bullied character's name]'s job, or is it the job of the other students in the class? What should they do to fix it? Do we have any students like [bullied character's name] in our class? Is this how we want our class to be? And, what should we do to fix it?

A third, essential component of bullying prevention is making it easy for students to report bullying when it happens. Of course, it is best when students are comfortable enough to speak with a teacher, and tell what happened. However, savvy schools have also developed other strategies to make it easy for students to report bullying. In one school, a school psychologist visited the classroom wearing a pair of Mickey Mouse ears, explaining that her job was to listen when students had a problem that they needed help solving. Then, she placed the ears on top of a ballot box at the back of the classroom, and students were instructed to slip a note into the box if they needed to be listened to. Other classrooms have set aside a bit of time each week for a classroom meeting, when students can talk about the issues that they are struggling with in the classroom. Still other classrooms publish a classroom newsletter with an advice column, where students can ask and have answered questions about small problems or irritations that they encounter. Together, activities preparing adults to be more vigilant, prompting students to be more sensitive, and providing multiple opportunities for students to report bullying are instrumental in reducing rates of peer-on-peer bullying in many classrooms.

MANUALIZED INTERVENTIONS

A number of comprehensive, manualized interventions exist that promote students' social competence or reduce the severity or frequency of students' peer aggression and rule breaking. In many instances, the studies that examined the efficacy of these interventions were conducted under ideal situations, with sufficient staff and materials to ensure that the programs were carried out as planned and in schools that were carefully selected to match the demands of the intervention. For these reasons, it is not always certain that a manualized intervention will have the same effectiveness in any particular school setting where school resources, populations, and challenging recess problems could differ in important ways from the settings where the initial research had occurred. Consequently, even when a manualized intervention has been verified to be "evidence based," it is important to collect ongoing data to ensure that the intervention is also effective in the particular school where it is being applied and with that school's students. Examples of four manualized interventions are described here, followed by instructions for finding other interventions to fit a particular school's needs.

Olweus Bullying Prevention Program

One of the first and still the most prominent bullying prevention program, the Olweus program (Olweus, Limber, & Mihalic, 1999) was originally developed in Norway and much of the research demonstrating its efficacy was conducted in Scandinavia. It combines schoolwide, classwide, and individual components, all of which are coordinated by a Bullying Prevention Coordination Committee. A schoolwide anonymous student survey is used to assess the prevalence of bullying, the information from which is used during a day-long school conference to plan bullying interventions, which always include strategies to increase supervision of students in the school's bullying "hot spots." Antibullying rules are established and enforced in classrooms, and regular classroom meetings are held to discuss bullying incidents in the class. Other interventions are provided for students who are victims of bullying or engage in bullying, and their parents are included in these interventions. International research has demonstrated that students' reports of bullying are reduced and their descriptions of the classroom's social climate are higher as a result of the Olweus Bullying Prevention Program. Expenses of the program include fees to purchase the bullying survey and train teachers, costs of classroom materials, release time for the day-long conference, and staff time for coordinating and carrying out the program.

Promoting Alternative Thinking Strategies (PATHS)

One of the most prominent programs for preventing emotional problems and discouraging peer aggression, PATHS (Greenberg, Kusché, & Mihalic, 1998) is a multiyear elementary classroom curriculum that teaches students self-control and social competence. The curriculum is delivered three times per week in brief 20–30-minute lessons by teachers or other adults. All teachers are trained in a two- to three-day workshop, and they meet every other week with a consultant who is an expert in the curriculum. Carefully conducted research has demonstrated that students' self-regulation improves and rates of peer aggression are diminished in PATHS schools. Expenses for the program include per-student fees for program materials, teacher release time for training and biweekly meetings with the coordinator, and the staff time for coordinating and carrying out the program.

I Can Problem Solve (ICPS)

Originating in some of the earliest work on social cognition, the ICPS curriculum (Shure, 1997) promotes prosocial behavior by teaching students to think about the social problems that they encounter, consider alternative solutions for solving the problems, carefully consider the feelings and motives of themselves and the other student, and translate these cognitive strategies into more competent social behaviors with peers. Originally developed for very young children (ages 4 and 5), more recent versions of ICPS have been created for elementary students. Teachers use illustrations, role plays, and classwide interactions to teach the social problem-solving skills; social concepts are graded developmentally. Research has demonstrated that ICPS students are less impulsive, are better problem solvers, and have more effective peer relationships, even several years after the program has ended. Expenses of the program include the costs for duplicating classroom materials, training teachers, and staff time associated with coordinating and maintaining the program.

Strong Kids

The Strong Kids series (Merrell, Gueldner, & Tran, 2008) of graded classroom curricula extends from kindergarten through eighth grade and promotes students' social and emotional learning, including socially competent peer interactions. They are designed to be simpler to implement than comprehensive manualized interventions, but also require fewer resources. Each curriculum includes 10–12 brief (30-minute) lessons beginning with a series of lessons on managing feelings followed by lessons on systematic social problem-solving strategies, solving people problems, setting and working toward personal goals, and managing stress. The Strong Kids manuals are carefully written to guide classroom teachers through the lessons without significant amounts of additional training. Each lesson includes a review of prior concepts, instruction and guided practice in new skills, skill maintenance strategies, training in generalizing the skills to new situations, and student worksheets. Copy-ready activities are included in the manual, and tools to monitor students' progress are available online. Expenses associated with the program include purchase of a teacher manual for each classroom teacher, reinforced with a few hours of teacher training and time for meeting with a curriculum consultant.

FINDING MORE MANUALIZED INTERVENTION

Additional intervention programs to strengthen students' social competence become available each year as new research findings are released, and so the best way to identify

promising programs is to conduct a comprehensive Internet
search. Four key Web sites are useful for beginning this
search. First, the Center for Academic and Social Emotional
Learning (CASEL) leads a collaborative group of researchers
who examine various strategies for promoting students' social
and emotional well-being. The group's Web site (http://www.
casel.org) includes one section describing more than 20 programs meeting the CASEL criteria for excellence. Links are
provided to program Web sites, with additional information
about promising programs that have not yet been listed on
the site (http://www.casel.org/programs/selecting.php). The
UCLA Center for Mental Health Services in the Schools (http://
smhp.psych.ucla.edu) includes a variety of practitioner tools,
including an annotated bibliography of evidence-based interventions for children and adolescents. Additional resources
describe strategies for creating community and school support
for projects that promote children's mental health, for evaluating the impact of interventions and programs, and for realign-
ing services around the programs that work. The Center for the
Study and Prevention of Violence (http://www.colorado.edu/
cspv/) has established standards for the adequacy of intervention research, and lists "blueprint programs" that have met
these standards—many of which are school-based programs
to promote social competence or prevent aggression. Finally,
the U.S. Department of Education's What Works Clearinghouse
(http://ies.ed.gov/ncee/wwc/) lists intervention strategies that
have met its standards for high-quality intervention research;
programs related to social competence are included under its
section on character education.

SUMMARY

This chapter has described a variety of different ways to
strengthen classroom recess and school playgrounds—each of
which has been effective for some classes in some settings.
It would be tempting to simply list the strategies according
to type of problem—some strategies promote student friendships, others prepare students to resolve their conflicts with
classmates, and still others stop bullying from happening.
However, selection of the best strategy to use also depends on
the nature of the students involved, the characteristics of the
school and the adults who work there, and the playground his-
tory in that school and community. That is why the Resilient
Playgrounds procedures do not preselect the changes that

will be made to improve playgrounds but, instead, describe a data-based problem-solving strategy that engages teachers and students in carefully thinking about their class and ensures that local data will be used to plan for and evaluate interventions. Chapter 6 will describe action research and marketing strategies that can be used to build support for playground improvement efforts, and Chapter 7 describes three classroom examples of Resilient Playgrounds projects.

Six

Documenting the Impact of Resilient Playgrounds Projects

<hr />

A ny effort to make a playground resilient will be more effective if it has broad support from the families, school, school district, and community that surround a classroom. Recess improvement efforts gain the respect of these audiences, and the support that accompanies respect, given *recognition* that the efforts are *responsible* for noteworthy improvements that are *important* for children's *school success*. These four terms are deliberately italicized in the preceding sentence. Support builds for a project when it is evident to the audience that things have changed for the better (improvements), the improvements are of the type and size that matter (importance), the improvements are relevant to the core responsibilities of schools (school success), and all of these facts are clearly recognized by others. This recognition does not occur accidentally, and does not automatically accrue to any beneficial project. Instead, a combination of action research (providing evidence of the program's impact) and marketing (so that important audiences know about the evidence) is essential for creating support for change. This chapter will describe the essential elements of both action research and project marketing.

The need for broad administrative and community support is not always pressing. In some cases, efforts to refine classroom or school recess are entirely consistent with a school's values, and there is no need to justify the efforts. In other cases, the modifications that are made are minor and the impact is strong, so that no one questions whether it is worth the effort to make the recess changes. However, in those instances where resources are needed to implement important changes in playground and recess routines—including resources such as more staff time, sizable alterations to the playground, purchase of a manualized intervention curriculum, or purchase of equipment or materials—a concerted effort will need to be made to document the impact of the recess changes and to market these changes to key audiences.

ACTION RESEARCH

Action research is a special case of empirical research that is conducted by practitioners who immediately act upon the study's results to refine and strengthen the outcomes of their daily practices. It is distinct from other forms of research in which researchers cooperate with practitioners but are not themselves practitioners, formulate research questions that may not be immediately important to practice, disseminate findings to audiences who are not engaged in practice, and have relatively little impact on the daily practices of schools. Because action researchers are also practitioners, their results can hold powerful influence over recess routines and practice.

Within Resilient Playgrounds, action research can contribute essential answers to questions about whether particular recess changes are responsible for important improvements in children's school success. There are two parts to these questions: Has recess improved? And did the playground changes cause the improvements?

The data-based problem-solving steps described in Chapter 4 are a form of action research—collecting data about students' recess experiences and using that data to refine and strengthen recess routines and practices. This is an example of a very simple but not very powerful research design called a *pre-post design*. Information is collected before a change is made and collected again after a change is made, and the difference between the two times can be used as a rough estimate of the impact of the change. The shortcoming of a pre-post design is that it never really proves *what* caused an improvement—it simply establishes that the improvement occurred.

For example, consider an eighth grade class that added more games to the lunchtime recess in an effort to reduce the number of aggressive incidents that occurred on the playground. Their data showed that, indeed, playground fighting did drop dramatically, and as a result, fewer students in the class were given 3-day suspensions for playground incidents. Still, it is possible that something else occurred during that interval to cause the drop in fighting. Perhaps a particularly aggressive student moved out of the district and so was no longer starting fights at lunchtime. Or, a new playground supervisor might have been hired who was much more effective in monitoring and interrupting students' aggressive behavior. Maybe a speaker from a local police station had convinced parents to reinforce playground courtesy. A very simple pre-post design, like the one used in this example, can show whether there have been changes in students' playground behaviors but may not be able to show what caused those changes to occur.

There are other practical research designs that provide more convincing answers to questions about the causes of recess improvements (Barlow, Nock, & Hersen, 2008). The simplest of these is a reversal design that can be used whenever the changes made in recess routines can be undone. Using this design, recess data would first be collected for several days without any changes being made (the baseline). Then, the planned changes in recess routines would be made for several more days while data continued to be collected. Next, those changes would be withdrawn for several more days, while data continued to be collected (the "reversal" phase). Finally, the planned changes would be reinstated while data continued to be collected. The reversal design is sometimes called an ABAB design, where *A* refers to the baseline and reversal phases during which no changes are made in recess routines and *B* refers to the phases where recess routines are changed according to the plan. This design can show whether the recess changes are responsible for the improvements if improvements are evident whenever the changes are in place (the B phases) and are not evident when no changes were made (the A phases).

Still, reversal designs cannot be used when the planned changes in recess routines cannot be undone. If a planned change was to add tetherball and foursquare games to the playground, it could be undone by keeping the balls locked up during the reversal phase. If a planned change was that playground supervisors would stand in a different place or would give out small tokens for good recess behavior, it could be undone by instructing the playground supervisors to return to their familiar ways of monitoring recess. However, if a planned change was to teach students how to play different games, it is impossible to "unteach" what students have already learned— and a reversal design would not be possible with this kind of change.

Whenever a reversal design can be used to evaluate changes in recess routines, it is also possible to use a compared treatments design. The principle difference occurs in the third phase: After collecting recess data for several days without making any changes (the baseline), and then making planned changes in recess routines (a B phase), a different set of recess changes is made in the third phase (a C phase). By alternating back and forth between the two sets of recess changes, it is possible to compare their different impact. For example, a compared treatments design could be useful for comparing two different kinds of recess supervision routines: catching students being good or coaching students in new games to play. With limited supervision resources, it could be very important to know whether one of these practices is more effective than the other.

If recess changes, once made, simply cannot be withdrawn, a multiple baseline design might be needed to prove that the changes are worthwhile. In this design, the changed recess procedures are made using a staggered schedule across different classrooms, different recess periods, or different behaviors. Recess data are then inspected to see whether recess improvements for each class, period, or behavior coincide in time with when the recess changes were made. Consider an elementary school in which a physical education teacher is systematically teaching students more games that they can play on the recess playground. With a multiple baseline design, the teacher would first gather baseline recess data to describe what recess was like before any changes are made. Then the games could be taught to the third graders while recess data continued to be collected for the third, fourth, and fifth grade recesses. Two weeks later, the games could be taught to third and fourth graders while recess data continued to be collected in all grades. Then, two weeks after that, the games could be taught to the fifth graders, too, while recess data continued to be collected. If recess improvements were obvious in each grade at the precise time when that grade began to learn the games, it would be convincing evidence that teaching the games had caused the recess improvements.

Multiple baseline designs can also be staggered across events. For example, a new recess supervision strategy could first be used during the morning recess, and then be used during both morning and lunchtime recess. Or, a multiple baseline design could be used across behaviors. For example, a team-choosing strategy might be used first for students who

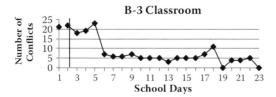

Figure 6.1.   Example of a simple data graph.

are playing soccer, then added two weeks later for students who are playing kickball, and so on.

In every case, these small-n research designs require that recess data be collected daily (or at least three or four times a week) so that enough data are available to show a trend in the recess improvements when phases are only a few weeks long. It is not always practical to collect multi-item survey data, like the ClassMaps Survey, (see Figure 4.2) that often. Too much time would be spent in analyzing and graphing the data, and students would tire of answering the same 19 questions every week. In most cases, then, only a single ClassMaps subscale is used for regular data, or other kinds of data are collected and graphed. Figure 4.4 listed a variety of simple data collection strategies that might be used in small-n research.

Regardless of the source of the data, data graphing is essential for evaluating the impact of a recess improvement program. For most of the evaluation designs described in this chapter, the most effective graphs are simple line graphs with dates along the horizontal axis and the results of the playground measure along the vertical axis. Transitions from one phase in the design to the next can be marked with dotted vertical lines. An example of a small-n data graph is displayed in Figure 6.1. These kinds of data graphs can easily display the project results to parents, other teachers, administrators, or school board members. More information about planning and carrying out small-n studies can be found in Barlow et al. (2008).

MARKETING RESULTS

If great improvements are made in a classroom's recess, but no one outside of the classroom knows that this has occurred, an important opportunity for advocacy has been lost. Students' families are the most important audience for information about a Resilient Playgrounds project. They can contribute to recess change efforts by reinforcing the changes during their conversations with children in the home. In some cases, changes that are made in the school could also be made in the home. For example, when a fourth grade put together a list of strategies for protecting themselves from bullying, families could remind children to use the same strategies in the neighborhood. Also, families are powerful advocates for resources and support from a school's administration and leadership, particularly when they are convinced that a program or change carries important benefits for their children.

One message is most important for families of a classroom's students: This project helps my child become more content, have more friends, or be more successful at school. Consequently, information that is provided to families should emphasize the results for their students as well as describe what the changes are and how their students are helping with the project. Graphs of the recess data will be most interesting to families if they are accompanied by anecdotes that tell different students' experiences and benefits.

Even very stressed and busy families pay attention to information that the students themselves produce. Rather than the teacher writing a weekly letter for parents, students could create a weekly newsletter that they have written, typed into a formatting program, and printed off for parents. Newsletters that have photographs of the classroom's new recess games or graphs of the recess data will be even more appealing. Students, singly or in groups, could create posters describing the recess changes, or present information on their project at one of the parent–teacher organization meetings.

A slightly different message is important for the school administration and leadership. First, they are very interested in knowing about special projects that reflect well on the school, and that could be included in their own reports to community members and district leadership. Also, if a project has good results, they are interested in copying it into other classrooms or grades. Finally, if a project has costs (resources or approvals), they are interested in knowing whether the costs are justified by the project's benefits. Any information that is provided to families could be useful for the school administration, because it satisfies their first need for information that they could disseminate. In addition, they will want explanations of the recess changes that are made—new rules for the playground soccer game or instructions for a teasing form—so that they can easily hand these off to someone else who is interested. Like parents, school administrators will find graphs of recess data to be very attractive because these immediately illustrate the benefit that they must have to justify any costs.

Policy makers at the district, community, or state level are principally interested in the costs and the benefits of a program, and in knowing more about how these balance one another. In addition to describing the costs of the playground improvements in funds, staff time, instructional time, and other resources, it will be important to describe the costs saved by the program. For example, a reduction from an average of seven to an average of two students sent to the office during recess, when each office visit "costs" 7 minutes of a principal's time, would result in a savings of 35 minutes per day or 175 minutes per week—almost three hours. Thus, any program that required a couple of hours weekly of paraprofessional time would easily be justified. For policy makers, in particular, information about a program is most effective when it is summarized on a single side of a sheet of paper with liberal use of bulleted lists, graphs, and tables. Contact information for a program leader should be prominently displayed.

SUMMARY

Many Resilient Playgrounds projects will be noncontroversial and can be conducted without need for substantial additional resources. For these projects, it will be unnecessary to gather firm evidence that the recess improvements that were made are responsible for enhancing students' social competence or reducing recess problems. However, when it becomes necessary to prove that the project has been effective, and that the improvements are worth the time and effort that were spent, it is possible to use action research methods to build a strong case for the value of Resilient Playgrounds interventions. This evidence can subsequently be shared with key administrators and policy makers, contributing to the ongoing viability of the project and its strategies for recess improvements.

Seven

Case Examples

The following examples describe the application of the Resilient Playgrounds strategy in three very different settings: a fourth grade struggling with temporary playground facilities, a seventh grade team in which several students were too isolated, and a first/second grade multi-age classroom responding to bullying incidents. In each case, accommodations were made for the particular needs of the class and the specific goals that were set for the classroom. Also, in each case, students' valuable contributions to the recess planning are evident.

EXAMPLE 1: A FOURTH GRADE
THAT ARGUED AND TEASED

Mrs. Gervais' fourth grade class was struggling through a year in a temporary school while their permanent school underwent extensive remodeling and asbestos removal. Because the temporary school was so far from their home school, many of their friends' parents had option-enrolled them in another school for the year. As a result, many of the students were missing their very good friends from the year before. The temporary playground was "make do" at best—a large flat field that lacked such amenities as the tetherball, foursquare courts, climbing structures, and a concrete pad for jumping rope or bouncing balls. With few other choices, most fourth graders spent the recess playing soccer. The playground supervisors were having a difficult year as well. They were preoccupied with keeping track of the children as they spread out across the field, and with escorting children across the parking access road that ran between the building and the playground. The playground was some distance away from the building door, requiring that the supervisors manage all but the most extreme misbehavior on the playground without calling upon the office staff. By the end of recess, tempers had often short-circuited, and many children came back into the school cranky and unhappy.

Determined to make things better, Mrs. Gervais and her students embarked upon their own "recess reform" project. To begin, all of the students completed the anonymous ClassMaps Survey in mid-February. The resulting data (Figure 7.1) show that rates of peer conflict were particularly high. Fully 25% of the students reported that they *almost always* or *often* had difficulties with arguing, teasing, and even physical fighting. Just as important, an additional 50% of the students said that teasing and arguing were sometimes a problem. Fewer students said that physical fighting was sometimes a problem.

The class and teacher met together to talk about their data. It was clear from the survey results and the students' discussion that most of the conflict involved verbal aggression—teasing, arguing, and name-calling. Most of it happened on the playground, but occasionally it followed the students back into the classroom. They agreed that the teasing, in particular, had become a serious problem for the class. Sometimes, they thought, the teasing students didn't realize that they were hurting a classmate's feelings—perhaps some of the teasing was inadvertent and meant in fun but simply went too far. In other cases, the teasing was probably a sign that there was an underlying disagreement between the students—over the rules to a game, a possession, or an accidental injury. The class made a very simple plan to stop the teasing. First, if someone was teasing them and it was hurting their feelings, the students would say "Ouch" in a firm and loud voice to signal that the teasing was becoming a problem. Then, if that didn't stop the teasing, the teaser and the teasee would have to sit down together and talk about the problem. A "teasing form" was developed to lead the students through the conversation (see Figure 7.2). The teaser would fill out the top of the form, the teasee would fill out the bottom of the form, and once the form was completely filled out, both of them would have a list of ideas for preventing the teasing from happening again. (See Teasing Form in Appendix F and on the accompanying CD.)

The other topic that dominated the students' comments was the lunchtime soccer game, their frequent arguments over picking teams, and their disagreements about the rules. One student added in a discouraged voice, "By the time we finish arguing about the teams, we only get to play for about five minutes a day." Ultimately, the class settled on a plan for change with several parts. First, they decided to choose soccer teams

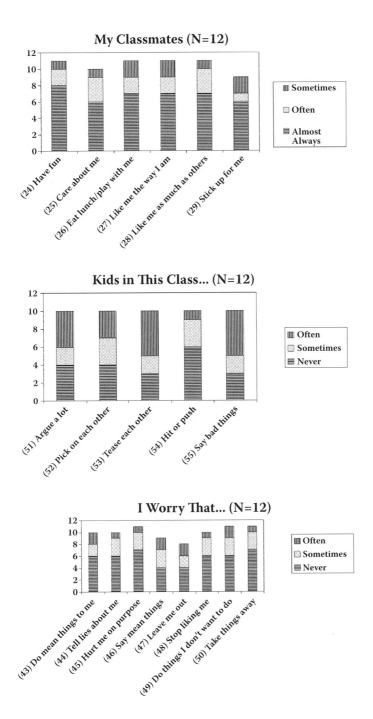

Figure 7.1. Beginning ClassMaps Survey data for Mrs. Gervais' class.

Who did the teasing? _____   **Who was teased?** _____

The Teaser	What did you do or say? _____
	
	_____
	
	Where did you do it? _____
	Why did you tease them? _____
	
	_____
	
	What did the other person do? _____
	
	_____
	
	Did teasing solve the problem? _____
	What are three things you might do instead the next time this happens?
	    1. _____
	    2. _____
	    3. _____
	What would you like to say to the person who you teased? _____
	
	_____

The One Who Was Teased	What did the teaser do or say? _____
	
	_____
	
	Where did it happen? _____
	Why did they tease you? _____
	
	_____
	
	What did you do about it? _____
	
	_____
	
	Did that solve the problem? _____
	What are three things you might do instead the next time this happens?
	    1. _____
	    2. _____
	    3. _____
	What would you like to say to the person who teased you? _____
	
	_____

Figure 7.2. Teasing form.

once a week and then use those same teams for the remainder
of the week. They added some "fairness" rules for choosing
teams: Certain "really good" soccer players had to be divided
evenly among the two teams, and everyone who wanted to
play had to be chosen for one team or the other. Next, they

decided to write a fourth grade soccer rule book. Mrs. Gervais volunteered to write the first draft, and then the students revised and refined the rules so that they fit the soccer game that they played at lunchtime. (Fourth graders were required to study expository writing, and so writing the soccer rule book was integrated into that curriculum.) Next, the students agreed that at least one student, each day, was needed as a referee. The class made a plan for training the referees, so that they knew the rules well. Finally, because all fourth graders in the school were outside at the same time, the class decided that they would try to convince the other fourth grades to join them in supporting the soccer rules.

Figure 7.3 is the written plan describing the changes that the class decided to make. For each change, the plan describes what would be done, who would do it, when it would happen, and where it would happen. The class record keeper kept track of whether or not each change was made by simply circling *yes*, *partly*, or *no* in a column along the right-hand side of the page. So that they could have some ongoing data on how well the plan was working, the class decided that they would each complete a "teasing thermometer" every Friday as they walked in from recess. One of the students was assigned to collect the sheets, compute the average teasing score, and record this on a graph that was hanging on a bulletin board next to the door. (Figure 7.4 shows the class's teasing thermometer, and Figure 7.5 shows the class's teasing graph. A copy of the teasing thermometer is included in Appendix G and on the *Resilient Playgrounds* CD.)

Four weeks later, the class recompleted the ClassMaps Survey and met together to talk about how well their plan was working. Their planning records showed that they had followed their plan faithfully, except that the teasing work-sheet had not been used even once. Students said that saying "Ouch" seemed to be enough to interrupt the teasing when it happened. Results of the ClassMaps Survey are shown in Figure 7.6. Results showed that most students in the class thought that arguing and teasing happened sometimes, but very few students reported that it happened often, and no one reported that it happened almost always. Their discussion and the survey results showed that rates of playground conflict had dropped and they were having much more fun during their recess. The soccer rulebook and team-selecting strategy had worked so well that several other classes were adopting them.

Classroom: Mrs. Gervais' Fourth Grade   Date: March 3, 2003

WHAT will change?	WHO will do it?	WHEN will it happen?	WHERE will it happen?	What is SUCCESS?	Did it happen?
1. Students will say, "Ouch," when someone is teasing and hurting their feelings.	All students	Whenever someone is teasing them	Wherever the teasing is happening	Teasing thermometer will average between 2 and 3	YES PARTLY NO
2. Students will fill out a teasing form if they teased someone else or were teased and the "Ouch" didn't fix it.	Students involved in teasing	Whenever the "Ouch" doesn't fix it; after recess	In the classroom		YES PARTLY NO
3. Lunchtime soccer rules will be written, including a knowledge quiz for referees and rules for choosing teams.	Mrs. Nash and the blue writing group	By March 17; during writing period	In the classroom during writing period	The written soccer rules	YES PARTLY NO
4. Soccer teams for the week will be chosen every Monday following the soccer rules (see 3).	All students who play soccer	Every Monday after reading	In the classroom	ClassMaps Kids in This Class data are 75% *often* and *almost always*	YES PARTLY NO
5. Two soccer referees will be chosen every Monday by drawing names from all who passed the rules quiz.	All students who passed the rules quiz	Every Monday after reading	In the classroom		YES PARTLY NO

Figure 7.3.   Written recess improvement plan for Mrs. Gervais' class.

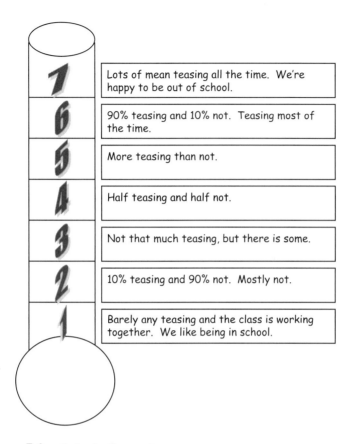

Figure 7.4.   The teasing thermometer.

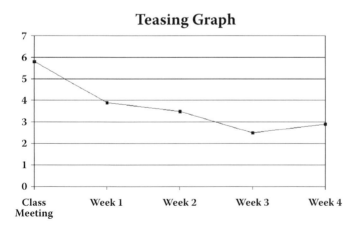

Figure 7.5.   The teasing graph of Mrs. Gervais' class.

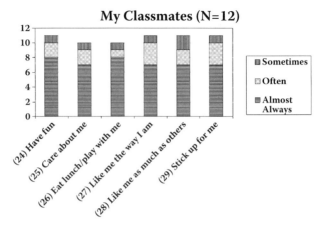

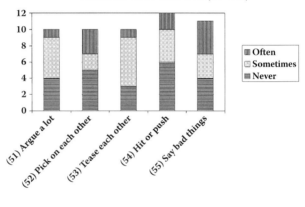

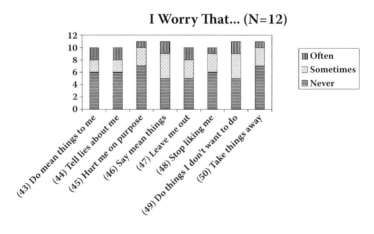

Figure 7.6. Ending ClassMaps Survey data for Mrs. Gervais' class.

EXAMPLE 2: A SEVENTH GRADE THAT
FORGOT TO INCLUDE SOME STUDENTS

The seventh grade–B (7B) team included four general education teachers, a special education teacher, and 102 seventh grade students. Situated at the edge of a medium-sized, Midwestern city, the school was experiencing a modest growth in enrollment as the aging neighborhood became very affordable for young, working-class families. Most of the students were able to walk to school from their homes, and many of them were latchkey children whose parents arrived home from work a couple hours after school was dismissed. The 7B teachers became concerned when a few parents began to ask about their child being too isolated, and spending the lunchtime break sitting alone.

The team began by holding a series of class meetings during the 30-minute homeroom that began each day. Each of the five teachers had 20 students who began the day with them, and they used this time for advising and study skills instruction. During the meetings, the teachers suggested that the students join them in a lunch break experiment in which they would gather some data about the students' friendships and conflicts during the 55-minute midday break, and then conduct a systematic study to improve the break while collecting data to evaluate how successful they had been. Students began by completing the anonymous ClassMaps Survey. (Results are shown in Figure 7.7.) As the teachers had suspected, almost 10% of the 7B students reported that they had few friends and spent the break alone. A closer examination showed that this problem was most pressing in the special education teacher's homeroom. Students assigned to the homeroom were those whose first class was Reading Basics—a catch-up reading skills class that included many of the team's students with disabilities. The 7B teachers became even more concerned that, for some reason, their students were excluding many of the students with disabilities from their friendships.

In another set of class meetings, the teachers shared the data graphs with the students and raised their questions about inclusion. The students uniformly agreed that the data were accurate, and some students were being routinely left out of their activities. Next, to emphasize the values of an inclusive society, the teachers showed the students a few short video clips from popular movies in which a student was being excluded, and the clips dramatized the very painful effects

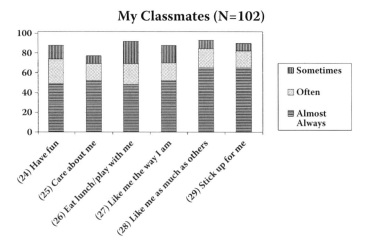

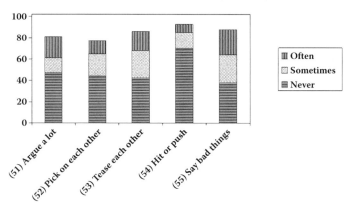

Figure 7.7.   Beginning ClassMaps Survey data for 7B.

that the isolation had on the student. After the clip, the teachers opened up three questions: What was causing the problem?
Whose responsibility was it to fix it? And what could be done
to fix it?

Although they were seeking the students' participation, the
7B teachers had already begun investigating some social values
curricula. They anticipated that they needed to raise the students' consciousness about the impact of exclusion and their
shared responsibility for confronting bias against disabilities.

However, in their discussion, the students gave a more practical explanation of the problem. They pointed out that they often decided what to do during lunch at the very beginning of the day, while they were sitting in their homerooms. They didn't intend to leave out the students in the Reading Basics homeroom, but because they weren't present in the room while recess was being planned, they didn't remember to include them. The students suggested that the Reading Basics homeroom should be disbanded, and its current students should be included in the other four 7B homerooms. Then, they would make a concerted effort to make sure that their new homeroom classmates were included in their planning. Finally, they suggested that they monitor the friendships in the team by read-ministering the six questions of the My Classmates subscale every Thursday (so that the students could count and graph the data for a Friday check-in meeting).

The students' plan is included in Figure 7.8, and a graph of their Thursday check-in data is included in Figure 7.9. Results show that there were important increases in the students' friendships. However, when all three ClassMaps subscales were administered six weeks later (see Figure 7.10), results showed that arguing continued to be a problem—and this became the subject of their next action plan.

EXAMPLE 3: BULLYING IN THE EARLY GRADES

Mr. Jimenez and Ms. Nash team taught 42 first and second graders, using a combination of flexible grouping, peer tutoring, and simple accommodations so that the students could learn in teams across the two grades. Healthy peer interactions were essential to their instructional strategies, and so the teachers were particularly concerned when the after-school crossing guard told them about instances where a few of their second graders were bullying some of the first graders.

Because the first graders in the class could not easily complete written surveys, the teachers gathered their data in a much simpler way. They chose three statements: I worry that other kids will do mean things to me; I worry that other kids will say mean things about me; I worry that other kids will try to make my friends stop liking me. Each question was posted on a bulletin board over three columns labeled *yes*, *sometimes*, and *no*. Then, they gathered the students together and read

Classroom: 7B's Friendship Plan   Date: November 2006

WHAT will change?	WHO will do it?	WHEN will it happen?	WHERE will it happen?	What is SUCCESS?	Did it happen?
1. Reading Basics homeroom will be disbanded, and students will be reassigned to the other four homerooms.	7B teachers	Next Monday	All classrooms	Students will report more friendships on the My Classmates subscale.	YES PARTLY NO
2. Assign an "ambassador" to each student from the former Reading Basics homeroom who will make sure the students are included.	7B students	Every day	In all four homerooms	Students will report more friendships on the My Classmates subscale.	YES PARTLY NO
3. Recollect the My Classmates data weekly from all students; count and graph the data.	Assigned 7B students from each homeroom	Every Thursday	In all four homerooms	The data are collected and ready for Friday check-in.	YES PARTLY NO
4. Check back each Friday to see how the plan is working.	7B teachers and assigned 7B students	Every Friday	In all four homerooms	Meetings will be held in all four homerooms.	YES PARTLY NO

Figure 7.8. 7B's written plan for improving the lunchtime break.

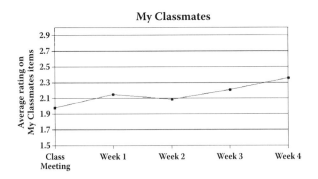

Figure 7.9. 7B's graph of My Classmates data.

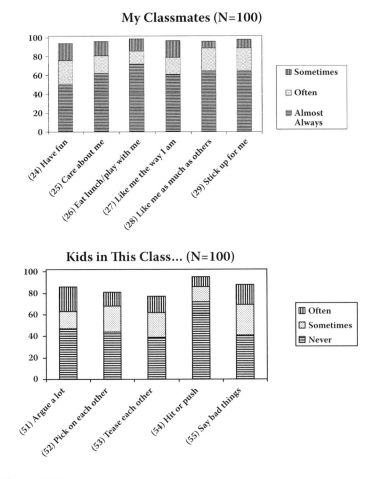

Figure 7.10. Ending ClassMaps Survey data for 7B.

each question in turn, talking briefly about what the question meant. Next, each student was given a square sticky note to stack underneath their answer. Once all students had stacked their notes, the class had constructed a simple bar graph that described the class's data.

Because the students had helped to make the graph, they were able to discuss their results with the teachers (results are shown in Figure 7.11). In this class, 24 students said *yes* or *sometimes* to the second question—they worried that other kids might say mean things about them. Also, 8 of the first graders and 4 of the second graders said *yes* or *sometimes* to the first question—they worried that other kids might do mean things to them.

So that the students could help decide what to do, the teachers divided them into three smaller groups. One group was the students who said that they had seen someone else being picked on. They met with Ms. Nash and talked about what they could do to stop the bullying when they saw it happening. They came up with three ideas: Say loudly, "Stop that. No bullying here." Get more friends and mob around the student who is being bullied, to help protect him or her. Or run quickly to tell a teacher. They wrote these ideas on several posters, and then the posters were placed around the room.

A second group was the students who said that they had been picked on. They met with Mr. Jimenez and talked about what they could do to protect themselves from bullying. They also came up with ideas: Say loudly, "Stop picking on me."

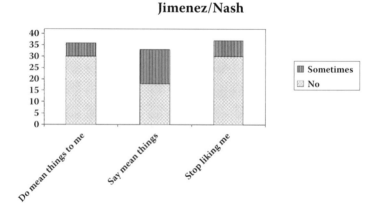

Figure 7.11. Bullying data for Mr. Jimenez' and Ms. Nash's first and second grade classroom.

Play with other friends, instead of playing alone. Play near where teachers are watching.

The last group was the students who said that they had picked on someone else. They also met with Mr. Jimenez, and they talked about what would stop them from bullying another student in the future. At the beginning of the discussion, they were quite indignant because they insisted that their victims had actually started it—they had gotten them into trouble earlier in the day, had taken cuts in the cafeteria, or had said something mean. At the top of their list of suggestions, they put, "Don't give us a reason for payback." Then, they admitted that they never picked on a student if an adult was watching, and so they added to the list, "Keep out of hidden corners." Toward the end of the discussion, they also said that bullying was fun, but not if their parents found out. The last suggestion on their list was notable because it did not require the victims of bullying to be responsible for stopping it: "Kids who bully should write a note to send home to their parents." Mr. Jimenez suggested that he and Ms. Nash would put a stamp on any bullying notes that students wrote, and the notes would be mailed home from the office.

The students' suggestions were included in a written bullying plan for the classroom, but it was obvious that teachers and other adults also needed to confront the bullying directly. They added two more steps to the plan: a schoolwide training in bullying that would alert all adults in the school to the problem of bullying and provide a common strategy for confronting it; and a "listening ear" box where students could "mail" reports to the teachers of bullying incidents that they experienced or observed. A copy of the classroom's written plan is included in Figure 7.12. One month later, the teachers repeated the bulletin board questions, and found that their plan appeared to have reduced the students' reports of classroom bullying. (Results are included in Figure 7.13).

SUMMARY

These examples of Resilient Playgrounds projects are very different from one another, not only in the students' age and grade but also in the problems that were identified and the strategies that were designed to address the problems. They illustrate the kinds of unexpected ideas or new insights that teachers and students can contribute when talking about the causes of their recess problems and their plans for change.

Classroom: 1st/2nd Class Bullying Play   **Date: January 2007**

WHAT will change?	WHO will do it?	WHEN will it happen?	WHERE will it happen?	What is SUCCESS?	Did it happen?
1. When someone is being bullied, both they and onlooking students will say, "Stop that. No bullying."	Students who are bullied or who see bullying happening	Every time	Anywhere in the school or playground	Students will report less bullying on the bulletin board questions.	YES PARTLY NO
2. When someone is being bullied, onlooking students will crowd around them to keep the bully away.	Students who see bullying happening	Every time	Anywhere in the school or playground	Students will report less bullying on the bulletin board questions.	YES PARTLY NO
3. When someone is being bullied, onlooking students will tell an adult right away.	Students who see bullying happening	Every time	Anywhere in the school or playground	Students will report less bullying on the bulletin board questions.	YES PARTLY NO
4. When someone is being bullied, they will move to play with other friends and play near where adults are watching.	Students who are bullied	Every time	Anywhere in the school or playground	Students will report less bullying on the bulletin board questions.	YES PARTLY NO
5. When students are bullied or see someone else bullied, they will put a note in the "listening ear" box to report what happened.	Students who are bullied or onlooking students	Whenever bullying happens	On the "listening ear" box by the classroom door	Teachers will find bullying notes in the box.	YES PARTLY NO
6. Teachers will tell every adult in the building what to do if they see a student being bullied.	Mr. Jimenez and Ms. Nash	The next school faculty meeting and school staff meeting	In the school library	Adults in the school will stop bullying when they see it.	YES PARTLY NO

Figure 7.12. Written recess improvement plan for the first and second grade classroom.

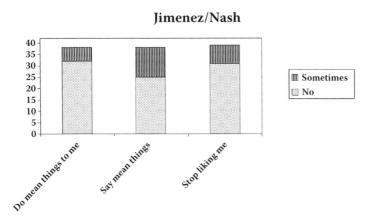

Figure 7.13.   Ending bullying data for the first and second grade classroom.

Classroom data were useful in focusing the fourth graders' attention on teasing and directing the 7B team's attention to student friendlessness. Examples of the students' critical contributions to problem solving are also evident: in the fourth graders' suggestions that it can be hard to notice that a classmate's feelings had been hurt, and that choosing soccer teams was a major recess irritation; in the 7B students' observation that the Reading Basics homeroom was contributing to the segregation of students with disabilities; and in the second graders' explanation of the role of paybacks in prompting bullying. One final insight is evident in a review of the end-of-project data describing each classroom: In most cases, the plans for change did not always fully "fix" the problem. However, they did make recess much better—a difference that might not have been evident without the data describing recess improvements. In Chapter 8, ten valuable resources for designing and carrying out Resilient Playgrounds projects will be described.

Eight

Top 10 Valuable Resources for Resilient Playgrounds

Classwide or schoolwide efforts to make playgrounds more resilient are ambitious undertakings, and may require more guidance than can fit into a single handbook. To help, this chapter describes the 10 resources that we have found to be most useful when carrying out playground projects.

1. Pellegrini, A. D. (2005). *Recess: Its role in education and development.* Mahwah, NJ: Lawrence Erlbaum.

For a detailed response to the critics who advocate for eliminating recess, consult Pellegrini's meticulously documented examination of the recess debate, the place of recess in U.S. schools, and the ways in which recess promotes children's social development and classroom success. Like most of his work, this book is firmly grounded in sound empirical research and comprehensive theories of social development. At the same time, it is a good read—it is clearly written, generously sprinkled with examples, and easily understood by educators and parents even if they have no prior experience with developmental research. This book provides ample rebuttals for any school district meeting debating the relevance of recess.

2. U.S. Consumer Product Safety Commission. (2008, April). *Public playground safety handbook.* Retrieved December 12, 2008, from http://www.cpsc.gov

This handbook was written for playground designers and administrators with oversight over the facilities and grounds where students spend their recess periods. It provides a highly detailed description of the characteristics of safe play structures and playgrounds, with an explanation of the hazards posed by structures that violate the safety standards, and strategies for modifying structures or grounds to bring them into compliance. Its easy-to-understand language makes the handbook a useful tool for anyone with playground responsibilities, and its clear diagrams and designs make the standards easy to apply to existing playgrounds.

3. GamesKidsPlay.net. (n.d.). *Welcome to GamesKidsPlay. net*. Retrieved August 5, 2009, from http://www.games kidsplay.net

There are many different Web sites describing children's games, and these change regularly. However, the GamesKidsPlay Web site has a large and useful mix of familiar childhood games, modified games that effectively accommodate students' different styles and abilities, and unfamiliar games from other cultures or continents. Sufficient information is provided about every game so that it could be played the following day on the playground.

4. Bailey, G. (2001). *The ultimate playground and recess game book*. Camas, WA: Educator's Press.

There are many different popular-press books on playground games, but this one stands out because it provides a very extensive description of outdoor games that pull students into vigorous play. Familiar games like dodgeball and tag have been modified to use foam balls or flags so that they are safe to play without sacrificing the fun.

5. Ladd, G. W. (2005). *Children's peer relations and social competence: A century of progress*. New Haven, CT: Yale University Press.

Recess is inextricably bound up in students' developing social competence and the interactions that they create with classmates and other peers. Ladd's book summarizes the empirical research on students' social competence, describing and interpreting it in a way that makes its implications for school practices very clear. Chapters are very pragmatically organized around topics such as "making friends and being accepted in peer groups" and "peer victimization is investigated as another aspect of children's peer relations." Its emphasis on the adequacy of empirical support and on the methodological dilemmas faced by researchers makes this book a challenging read for practitioners who are more than a few years away from their university studies. However, its utter dependability and accuracy recommend it as a key reference to consult when searching for more information on particular aspects of recess.

> 6. Developmental Studies Center. (1996). *Ways we want our class to be: Class meetings that build commitment to kindness and learning.* Oakland, CA: Author.

This deceptively small and simple handbook provides a very student-sensitive description of classroom meetings and the strategies that make them successful. It begins with a 43-page explanation of the principles, contexts, and facilitation strategies underlying effective meetings among teachers and students, and then provides 14 examples of meetings that could be held on specific topics. Together these explanations make it easy to step into the role of leading a meeting and are convincing evidence of the meetings' worth.

> 7. Crone, D. A., Horner, R. H., & Hawken, L. S. (2004). *Responding to problem behavior in schools: The Behavior Education Program.* New York: Guilford.

Careful examinations of playground discipline records almost always show that a few students are responsible for well over half of the serious rule-breaking behaviors. The Behavior Education Program works to improve the schoolwide behavior of these difficult students, using a check-in and check-out procedure that is very similar to that used in most school-based programs for students with behavior problems. Very clear instructions are provided for creating the behavioral progress reports with students and systematically monitoring them, and realistic guidance is provided describing the resources that are necessary for successfully implementing this kind of program.

> 8. Bear, G. G., Cavalier, A. R., & Manning, M. A. (2005). *Developing self-discipline and preventing and correcting misbehavior.* Boston: Pearson Education.

Successful recess depends in part upon successful discipline strategies that discourage recess misbehavior, and Bear and his colleagues provide a very balanced explanation of student-directed as well as contingency management strategies for discipline. In particular, the chapters on "preventing misbehavior with effective classroom management" and "developing social and moral problem solving" could easily become the basis for training playground supervisors or refining schoolwide reinforcement of playground rules.

9. Corsaro, W. A. (2003). *We're friends, right? Inside kids' culture.* Washington, DC: Joseph Henry.

Corsaro's book brings alive vivid memories of what it was truly like to be a young child with friends, and reminds readers of the power of the kid society that students live within. Punctuated with frequent examples of his own dialogue with young children, he explores issues of sharing, making and keeping friends, playing make-believe, and conflict. Although his specific examples may not transfer to any particular school classroom, they are convincing evidence that students do think differently about friendships than adults—and that recess improvement projects will benefit from the conversations with children that provide the kids' point of view about what happens on the playground and how to fix it.

10. Doll, B., Zucker, S., & Brehm, K. (2004). *Resilient classrooms: Creating healthy environments for learning.* New York: Guilford.

Chapter 4's action research model for strengthening school environments that underlies resilient playgrounds was also described, in more detail, in the *Resilient Classrooms* book. In this earlier book, you will find multiple alternative examples for displaying research data to students, including younger students, and for including students in the planning and decision making for classroom change.

Appendix A:
Resilient Playgrounds
Playground Safety Checklist

————————

☐ The playground has clearly defined boundaries.
☐ It is located away from traffic, or, at a minimum, there are high fences separating the playground from traffic.
☐ There is a direct walkway from the school onto the playground.
☐ Children do not walk across roads or parking lots to get to the playground.
☐ The playground is free of hazards like potholes, large rocks, broken glass, or other hazardous waste.
☐ Any grates or drainage culverts are well marked.

Playground equipment does not have

    ☐ sharp edges that could cut,
    ☐ moving parts that could pinch or crush,
    ☐ overhangs that could cause impact injuries, or
    ☐ openings that could entrap.

☐ Any climbing equipment has been designed to prevent children from jumping off.
☐ The playground surfaces are soft and shock-absorbing to cushion children during falls.
☐ The playground surfaces are heat deflecting so that they will not burn children, even on hot and sunny days.
☐ Swings are made from soft fabric and spaced so that other children do not readily walk in the path of moving swings.
☐ Sports fields are spaced so that other children are not accidentally hit by balls or other equipment from the game.
☐ Goal posts and boundaries are padded and flexible to avoid impact injuries.
☐ There are places on the playground that are shaded from the sun.

☐ There are clear safety rules that prohibit unsafe play on the playground.

☐ All playground supervisors know and enforce the safety rules.

☐ All students receive direct instruction in the safety rules.

Appendix B:
Resilient Playgrounds
Playground Supervision
Checklist

☐ There are sufficient numbers of adults supervising the playground (1 adult for 20–30 students).
☐ Playground supervisors locate themselves in places where they have good visibility of all areas of the playground.
    ☐ There are no "hidden" corners in the playground.
    ☐ Supervisors distribute themselves around the playground.
    ☐ Supervisor move continuously around their assigned areas.
    ☐ Supervisors scan continuously.
☐ Playground supervisors know the playground rules.
☐ Playground supervisors use consistent procedures for enforcing playground rules:
    ☐ Effective commands to stop minor rule violations
    ☐ Some form of on-the-playground time-out to interrupt more important rule violations
    ☐ Strategies for rewarding positive playground behaviors (e.g., raffle tickets or wrist loops)
☐ Playground supervisors can secure additional assistance (e.g., for accidents or very difficult behaviors) without leaving the playground.
    ☐ There are clear procedures that office staff or classroom teachers will follow to enforce playground rules when the efforts of playground supervisors are insufficient.
☐ Playground supervisors provide active supervision.
    ☐ They actively interact with the children and make comments on their activities.
    ☐ They praise the children for appropriate behavior.
    ☐ They may participate in the play.

☐ They prompt isolated children in how to join in the play.
☐ They discourage aggression.
☐ Children have been given direct instruction in the playground rules, procedures, and games.
  ☐ Recess workshops—tours of the playground with guided practice in the equipment and demonstration of playground rules and expectations (Todd et al., 2002).
  ☐ Classroom instruction in a common set of playground rules, routines, and expected behaviors (Lewis et al., 2002).

Appendix C:
Resilient Playgrounds
Promoting Playground
Play Checklist

- [ ] There are many different games for children to play.
  - [ ] There are sufficient numbers of games appropriate for early elementary students: swings, climbing equipment, sand boxes or digging, and areas for chase games.
  - [ ] There are sufficient numbers of games appropriate for later elementary students: four square, tether ball, Frisbee golf, soccer, jump rope, and kickball.
  - [ ] Games have not been compromised by poor design or limited availability of equipment.
- [ ] There is a mix of competitive games (rule based, like soccer, kickball, and basketball) and cooperative games (like jump rope, slides, and climbing games).
- [ ] There are sufficient numbers of games that can be played in very small groups (2–3 kids) for children who are easily intimidated.
- [ ] Many of the games provide vigorous physical exercise.
- [ ] Many of the games provide opportunities for children to take risks and build physical skills.
- [ ] There are sufficient numbers of games appropriate for children with limited athletic talents.
- [ ] There are sufficient numbers of games appropriate for children who use wheelchairs or have other forms of disabilities.
- [ ] Games are spread out across the playground, and there is enough space for children to play without crowding into each other.
- [ ] Children receive direct instruction in how to play the games.
- [ ] Recess is long enough for children to become engrossed in a game, but short enough so that they don't become bored again.

☐ There are occasional "game clinics," where one or more adults teach interested children how to play new games.

☐ Adults regularly join in and lead games with children.

Appendix D:
ClassMaps Survey 2007

Directions: These questions ask what is true about your class. For each question, circle the choice that is true for you. Do not put your name on the paper. No one will know what your answers are.

I am a: ☐ Boy / male   ☐ Girl / female   I am in the _____ grade.

Believing in Me

1. I can do my work correctly in this class.
   Never   Sometimes   Often   Almost always

2. I can do as well as most kids in this class.
   Never   Sometimes   Often   Almost always

3. I can help other kids understand the work in this class.
   Never   Sometimes   Often   Almost always

4. I can be a very good student in this class.
   Never   Sometimes   Often   Almost always

5. I can do the hard work in this class.
   Never   Sometimes   Often   Almost always

6. I can get good grades when I try hard in this class.
   Never   Sometimes   Often   Almost always

7. I know that I will learn what is taught in this class.
   Never   Sometimes   Often   Almost always

8. I expect to do very well when I work hard in this class.
   Never   Sometimes   Often   Almost always

My Teacher

9. My teacher listens carefully to me when I talk.
   Never   Sometimes   Often   Almost always

10. My teacher helps me when I need help.
    Never   Sometimes   Often   Almost always

11. My teacher respects me.
    Never   Sometimes   Often   Almost always

12. My teacher likes having me in this class.

    Never   Sometimes   Often   Almost always

13. My teacher makes it fun to be in this class.

    Never   Sometimes   Often   Almost always

14. My teacher thinks I do a good job in this class.

    Never   Sometimes   Often   Almost always

15. My teacher is fair to me.

    Never   Sometimes   Often   Almost always

Taking Charge

16. I want to know more about the things we learn in this class.

    Never   Sometimes   Often   Almost always

17. In this class, I can guess what my grade will be when I turn in my work.

    Never   Sometimes   Often   Almost always

18. I work as hard as I can in this class.

    Never   Sometimes   Often   Almost always

19. I find and fix my mistakes before turning in my work.

    Never   Sometimes   Often   Almost always

20. I learn because I want to and not just because the teacher tells me to.

    Never   Sometimes   Often   Almost always

21. When the work is hard in this class, I keep trying until I figure it out.

    Never   Sometimes   Often   Almost always

22. I know the things I learn in this class will help me outside of school.

    Never   Sometimes   Often   Almost always

23. I can tell when I make a mistake on my work in this class.

    Never   Sometimes   Often   Almost always

My Classmates

24. I have a lot of fun with my friends in this class.

    Never   Sometimes   Often   Almost always

25. My friends care about me a lot.

    Never   Sometimes   Often   Almost always

26. I have friends to eat lunch with and play with at recess.

    Never   Sometimes   Often   Almost always

27. I have friends that like me the way I am.

    Never   Sometimes   Often   Almost always

28. My friends like me as much as they like other kids.

    Never   Sometimes   Often   Almost always

29. I have friends who will stick up for me if someone picks on me.

    Never   Sometimes   Often   Almost always

Following the Class Rules

30. Most kids work quietly and calmly in this class.

    Never   Sometimes   Often   Almost always

31. Most kids in this class listen carefully when the teacher gives directions.

    Never   Sometimes   Often   Almost always

32. Most kids follow the rules in this class.

    Never   Sometimes   Often   Almost always

33. Most kids in this class pay attention when they are supposed to.

    Never   Sometimes   Often   Almost always

34. Most kids do their work when they are supposed to in this class.

    Never   Sometimes   Often   Almost always

35. Most kids in this class behave well even when the teacher isn't watching.

    Never   Sometimes   Often   Almost always

Talking With My Parents

36. My parents and I talk about my grades in this class.

    Never   Sometimes   Often   Almost always

37. My parents and I talk about what I am learning in this class.

    Never   Sometimes   Often   Almost always

38. My parents and I talk about my homework in this class.

    Never   Sometimes   Often   Almost always

39. My parents help me with my homework when I need it.

    Never   Sometimes   Often   Almost always

40. My parents and I talk about ways that I can do well in school.

    Never   Sometimes   Often   Almost always

41. My parents and I talk about good things I have done in this class.

    Never   Sometimes   Often   Almost always

42. My parents and I talk about problems I have in this class.

    Never   Sometimes   Often   Almost always

I Worry That . . .

43. I worry that other kids will do mean things to me.

    Never   Sometimes   Often   Almost always

44. I worry that other kids will tell lies about me.

    Never   Sometimes   Often   Almost always

45. I worry that other kids will hurt me on purpose.

    Never   Sometimes   Often   Almost always

46. I worry that other kids will say mean things about me.

    Never   Sometimes   Often   Almost always

47. I worry that other kids will leave me out on purpose.
    Never   Sometimes   Often   Almost always

48. I worry that other kids will try to make my friends stop liking me.
    Never   Sometimes   Often   Almost always

49. I worry that other kids will make me do things I don't want to do.
    Never   Sometimes   Often   Almost always

50. I worry that other kids will take things away from me.
    Never   Sometimes   Often   Almost always

Kids in This Class

51. Kids in this class argue a lot with each other.
    Never   Sometimes   Often   Almost always

52. Kids in this class pick on or make fun of each other.
    Never   Sometimes   Often   Almost always

53. Kids in this class tease each other or call each other names.
    Never   Sometimes   Often   Almost always

54. Kids in this class hit or push each other.
    Never   Sometimes   Often   Almost always

55. Kids in this class say bad things about each other.
    Never   Sometimes   Often   Almost always

Appendix E:
Resilient Playgrounds
Plan for Change Form

Classroom _____   Date _____

WHAT will change?	WHO will do it?	WHEN will it happen?	WHERE will it happen?	What is SUCCESS?	Did it happen?
1.					YES PARTLY NO
2.					YES PARTLY NO
3.					YES PARTLY NO
4.					YES PARTLY NO
5.					YES PARTLY NO

Appendix F:
Teasing Form

Who did the teasing? _____   **Who was teased?** _____

The Teaser	What did you do or say? _____
	
	 _____
	
	 Where did you do it? _____
	 Why did you tease them? _____
	
	 _____
	 What did the other person do? _____
	
	 _____
	 Did teasing solve the problem? _____
	 What are three things you might do instead the next time this happens?
	   1. _____
	   2. _____
	   3. _____
	 What would you like to say to the person who you teased? _____
	
	 _____

The One Who Was Teased	What did the teaser do or say? _____
	
	 _____
	 Where did it happen? _____
	 Why did they tease you? _____
	
	 _____
	 What did you do about it? _____
	
	 _____
	 Did that solve the problem? _____
	 What are three things you might do instead the next time this happens?
	   1. _____
	   2. _____
	   3. _____
	 What would you like to say to the person who teased you? _____
	
	 _____

Appendix G:
Teasing Thermometer

7 — Lots of mean teasing all the time. We're happy to be out of school.

6 — 90% teasing and 10% not. Teasing most of the time.

5 — More teasing than not.

4 — Half teasing and half not.

3 — Not that much teasing, but there is some.

2 — 10% teasing and 90% not. Mostly not.

1 — Barely any teasing and the class is working together. We like being in school.

Appendix H:
The Parents'
Friendship Meeting:
A Parent Information
Curriculum for Parents of
Children Without Friends

LEADING THE PARENTS' FRIENDSHIP MEETING

The Parents' Friendship Meeting is for parents of children who are having difficulty forming or maintaining satisfying friendships with peers. Its goal is to enhance the quality and quantity of children's friendships when children have few or no close friends, are unable to play with friends for extended periods, are unable to resolve disagreements with friends, aren't asked to play by other children, are turned down when asking other children to play, are uninterested in seeking out friendships, or derive little or no enjoyment from playing with friends.

Each unit of the Parents' Friendship Meeting follows a standard format. First, information from the previous meeting is reviewed; parents report on their experiences in practicing the previous meeting's strategy, and other parents comment or assist when a parent reports difficulty practicing that strategy. Second, the new information that will be presented to parents is summarized in 5–10 minutes. The new information is discussed, and parents' questions about the new information are answered. Third, one or more discussion questions are posed about the new information, and each parent has an opportunity to participate in the discussion. Finally, using a written activity, parents apply that meeting's topic to their child. The seven Parents' Friendship Meetings proceed systematically through six topics:

Meetings 1 and 2: What's normal in children's friendships?
Meeting 3: Getting your child to talk to you about friendships

Meeting 4: Children's ability to understand the other child
Meeting 5: Helping your child see the other child's point
of view
Meeting 6: Helping children solve friendship problems
Meeting 7: Systematically setting goals

Often, leaders of the parents' meeting will plan one final meeting to review all six topics and to help parents plan for their continuing support of children's friendships.

Through their participation in the Parents' Friendship Meeting: (a) Parents receive *instruction* in theories and research that describe children's friendships and the social interactions of children without friends. Although parents come to the meetings with a sophisticated understanding of adult friendships, they frequently don't understand that their child's reasoning about friends and social relationships is different from their own. (b) Parents are repeatedly engaged in activities that require them to *apply this information* to their own child and to their own parenting. Knowledge about children's friendship skills will only be useful to parents once they apply it to their own child's experience. (c) Parents are taught *friendship-enhancing strategies* and are encouraged to practice these during the intervals between meetings. The friendship-enhancing strategies used in the meeting flow naturally from the instruction and the applications that are provided. (d) Parents are encouraged to *reflect* upon this practice in a way that provides them with a fuller understanding of their own children's friendships. The discussion from this review allows parents to assist each other in resolving problems that occur.

The ultimate intent of the meetings is that parents will continue using the friendship strategies with their children after completing the last meeting.

TOPIC 1: WHAT'S NORMAL
IN CHILDREN'S FRIENDSHIPS?

Adults know what a friend is: A friend is someone who you can trust not to tell a secret. A friend is someone who notices when you need help and who comes through in a pinch. A friend is someone who still likes you after seeing you at your worst. A friend won't disappear when times are hard. A friend is someone you can talk to about anything and know they'll listen. A friend is someone you do favors for, and who does favors for you. We could continue this list and as we did, we would be describing the adult concept of "friend."

Children don't think about friends in the same way that adults do. As they grow in age and understanding, they gradually develop the adult concept of friend, one piece at a time. It isn't usually until midadolescence that the child's "friend" is similar to the adult's. Many times as we try to help children with friendships, we forget that the child's "friend" means something different.

Preschool children choose friends who they see every day. A friend is someone who is convenient and available to play. Friends are someone you have a good time with. Friends share toys. If a fight erupts or if a convenient friend moves away, the preschooler's friendship ends. Preschoolers don't recognize the friendship as a lasting relationship that can survive a separation or disagreement. Ask preschoolers to identify their friends, and they will invariably mention neighbors or classmates that they see every day.

Once children are school-aged, they choose friends who help them. Friends enjoy doing what they do and share common interests. Friends share their thoughts and feelings with each other. Sometimes, but not always, school-aged children understand that friendships are strong enough to last through times apart or a single fight. Six-year-old Martha, although upset when her best friend Tina moved out of state, insisted that Tina was still her best friend. She explained that they both liked hamsters and jumped rope, and had never had a fight while playing. School-aged friendships end with a lapse in understanding or loyalty.

By 11 or 12, children develop a more mature understanding of a friendship. A friendship is a relationship rather than an enjoyable activity. Older children realize that a friendship relationship is two-way: The way they act toward friends will help determine how they are treated. Eleven-year-old Scott also had a best friend with whom he spent most of his free time. The friendship weathered frequent fights because, within a few days, each boy would approach the other and offer a favor or compliment. As Scott explained, "He isn't always nice, but he's a good friend. He's the only one that plays 'Dungeons and Dragons,' and he puts up with me when I'm mad."

What do children learn from friendships? Friendships provide children with opportunities to practice getting along with other people. Children learn how to present their best face to other people. They learn how to match their own behavior to what other people expect of them. They learn how to figure out what other people are thinking about them, and how to create a favorable impression.

Friendship is also a shelter within which children can make social mistakes. They can play pranks on a friend without hurting a friendship. They can have a bad day, and a friend will understand. They can talk about forbidden subjects with a friend. They can practice using and avoiding insults. Watch a group of children on a playground. They'll call each other *slowpoke* and *scaredy cat*. They'll "accidentally" bump into one another, and push one another away from a tree or base. Adults sometimes wonder why they continue to play together, when play becomes that rough. Children sometimes wonder why adults can't take it all in stride like they do. The games make more sense when we think of them as practice in "taking the world in stride."

Differences Between Kids Who Have Friends and Kids Who Don't

How do children who don't have friends differ from those who do? We study friendships in classrooms by asking questions of the entire class. Members of the class may be asked to write down the person who works the hardest, who they'd like on their baseball team, who they would most like to study with, or who they would invite to a birthday party. It is then possible to explore the friendships formed in the classroom by noting who is named as a desired friend, who is named as a problem, and who is not named at all.

In any classroom group, 5% to 10% are not named as a friend by any other child. Between 12% and 20% are named as a friend by only one other child. Most of these children are not actively disliked—they're simply overlooked. It has been difficult to discover how these overlooked children are different from popular children. Some observers suggest that overlooked children are not likely to walk away in the face of a disagreement. And they are likely to hover nearby watching a group of playing children, rather than joining in. Jason is an example. He complained to his parents that he had few friends. By watching Jason on the playground, it was easy to see why. He often hung out on the edges of a group. When they played a game, he stood and watched. When asked why, he explained that he couldn't play well or that it wasn't a game he liked to play. But the end result was that Jason spent most recess periods watching from the sidelines.

A single child will only identify one or two classmates as actively disliked. Some children who are disliked are most likely to be unkind to other children. They say insulting things more often, and are more likely to hit or kick another child. Disliked children are unlikely to compromise when involved in disagreements. They are not as likely to suggest a game or suggest playing to another child. Jenny is an example of this kind of disliked child. If you stood in the hallway outside her room while she played with a friend, you'd need both hands to count the disagreements. She didn't want to play Candyland. Mary wasn't allowed to touch her hamster. It wasn't fair when Mary rolled the dice first. Jenny won most of the arguments, but Mary left and went home an hour early.

There is a second kind of child who is actively disliked. These are the children who are strange or unusual. They're frequently teased because of their unusual behavior, and because other children can't understand them. Sometimes these children can become more accepted when other children are given reasons for their strangeness.

Children who are well liked typically spend much more of their day playing with friends. They will suggest playing more often, and will almost always agree when asked by a friend to play. Liked children will let the other child choose the activity as long as it permits playing together. They are usually good communicators, and they both understand and are understood by their friends.

There is another important difference between children who have friends and those who don't. Children with lots of friends usually treat their friends more kindly than those who don't have friends. This becomes obvious when we observe well-liked children in the classroom or at recess. They are more likely to

- say kind things to friends,
- share with friends,
- sympathize with a friend who is hurt,
- rescue a friend who is being chased,
- defend a friend being teased,
- compliment a friend, and
- give small gifts to friends.

All children will encounter disagreements when they interact with friends. The differences occur in how children settle their problems with friends. Well-liked children are more likely to suggest a compromise, and will give up some of what they want to stay friends. They will take the time to explain why they want to play a certain game, or to use a certain rule. And they are more likely to listen when the other child explains their side.

Well-liked children are believed to help others more than their unliked peers. Some differences between helping children and those who don't help can be found in the way they were disciplined. Parents of helping children usually use a rational approach to discipline. They give explanations for discipline, and point out the harmful consequences of their child's misbehavior on others. They rarely try to make their child feel guilty, and use mild rather than severe discipline. Children need to be taught how to be kind, as well as how not to be unkind. Parental reasoning, modeling, and concrete suggestions are most effective in showing your child how to be considerate. In many cases, however, children who don't help don't intend to be unkind. They simply don't notice that another child is in trouble.

DISCUSSION QUESTIONS

1. Think about a favorite friend from when you were 10. What was it about this friend that you found attractive? Why do you think the friend chose you?
2. Remember any friend you had that your parents disapproved of. What was it about the friend that you found attractive? What did your parents find objectionable?
3. Can you remember a recent incident where you and your child disagreed about a friendship? Were there

differences in the way you and your child thought about friendships that caused the disagreement?

4. Is your child actively disliked, overlooked, or well liked? Can you explain why this might be so?

TOPIC 1 ACTIVITY: UNDERSTANDING YOUR CHILD

1. Imagine that your child and Louis, a neighbor, are playing Monopoly. They begin to disagree over a rule. Louis has always placed any fines or fees into a kitty in the middle of the board; a person who lands on FREE PARKING collects any money in the kitty. Your child has never used a kitty, and thinks Louis made up the rule. What would your child do?

___ Give in quickly and go on with the game.
___ Argue about the rule without giving in.
___ Call Louis names like "cheater."
___ Suggest a compromise.
___ Quit the game.
___ Something else.

2. Imagine that a new student has joined your child's class at school. It's recess time, and most of the class is involved in a rough-and-tumble game of kickball. The new kid is hovering nearby and watches the class play, but makes no move to join. The new kid looks a bit sad, and shy. What would your child do?

___ Approach the new student and ask him or her to join.
___ Smile at the new student but walk by without saying anything.
___ Ask the new student to move to one side out of the way of the game.
___ Remark to a friend that the new kid is kind of strange.
___ Tease the new student, or call him or her a name.
___ Not notice the new kid.
___ Something else.

3. Imagine that your child's best friend has arrived at school angry because of a heated argument with parents. The friend doesn't answer your child's call of "Hello" and seems to turn away when asked to play. Finally, when the bell rings and the two run toward

the door of the school building, the friend accidentally bumps your child and then growls, "Watch out, will ya?" What would your child do?

___ Growl back, and let it grow into a fight.
___ Walk away, with feelings hurt.
___ Call the friend a name.
___ Ask the friend what's wrong.
___ Make a joke, and ignore the friend's crankiness.
___ Something else.

4. Imagine it's a friend's birthday and the friend is bragging about the computer program a grandmother sent. Your child knows that the child's grandmother rarely visits and never remembers to send birthday presents. Your child suspects that the friend is lying. What would your child do?

___ Call the child a liar.
___ Walk away and ignore the story.
___ Believe the story.
___ Get jealous of the present.
___ Something else.

5. Your child is acting in a play with several other children. At a key moment in the performance, one of the other children forgets their lines. The play is disrupted, and several of the children are angry with the one who forgot. What would your child do?

___ Get angry with the child who forgot.
___ Get angry with the rest.
___ Tell the forgetter that it's OK, everyone makes mistakes.
___ Walk away without saying anything.
___ Make a joke or make fun of the forgetter.
___ Something else.

TOPIC 2: GETTING YOUR CHILD TO TALK
TO YOU ABOUT FRIENDSHIPS

As children enter grade school, it becomes more and more difficult for parents to understand the kinds of problems children face each day. School-aged children are often reluctant to
talk about their school problems at home. To be practical, once
children enter school, family life becomes very rushed and it
is difficult to find a time for thoughtful conversation about a
problem. Moreover, many children assume that school is their
responsibility, and believe that they ought to be able to handle
school problems independently. Other children don't want to
get in trouble at home for what happens at school; they operate
on the theory that the less parents know, the better. Still other
children complain that parents don't understand about school
or the problems that happen there.

In fact, the children are right. When parents talk to them
about a problem, many of the things they say aren't very helpful. When parents are very concerned about a child's happiness, they want to solve the problem quickly. As a result, they
are likely to

- preach to their child about "good" ways to handle the
  problem,
- make suggestions about what the child should or ought
  to do,
- lecture or give the child logical reasons for handling
  the problem differently,
- criticize the way the child handled the problem in the
  first place,
- sympathize with the child for the mistreatment suf-
  fered at the hands of friends,
- interrogate the child about what exactly happened and
  why,
- try to kid around to help the child forget about the
  problem, and/or
- direct the child to do something the next day to solve
  the problem.

These seem like appropriate responses unless we think
about them from the child's perspective. Imagine that you
were in an automobile accident. You were making a left-hand
turn across traffic. A car across the intersection was turning
left too, and you didn't notice that another car was behind it,

crossing straight through into your path. You turned into the second car's side. After living through the police report and wrecker, you've arrived home and are trying to talk about the accident with a spouse. Would you want them to say any of the following?

"You never should turn across a lane of traffic until you have a clear view of it."

"You ought to be able to make a safe turn at your age."

"Whenever a car is in the left-turn lane, it's difficult to see around them. The safest way to proceed is to anticipate that other cars will be traveling in the far lanes."

"You're always so impatient to make your turn. If you would just slow down a little."

"That car had no business moving straight through the intersection. The police officer should have ticketed that driver for driving at unsafe speeds."

"Tell me again. Exactly where were you in the intersection? Had you edged your car into the far lane at the time the other driver entered the intersection? Exactly where was the car behind you?"

"There you go again. That's the fourth car you've totaled since we've been married. Aw come on, I'm only kidding."

"Tomorrow I want you to call the insurance agent and explain exactly what happened. Tell him..."

Children with friendship problems are having social accidents rather than traffic accidents, but they frequently come home feeling angry, nervous, worried, and traumatized.

Parents can be a valuable resource for children with friendship problems if they can respond to these social accidents in helpful ways. First, it is important to open the door to a conversation by inviting the child to say more. Then, to keep the door open, the parent must listen closely and carefully to what the child is saying. When parents make themselves available to a child to talk, and then listen well, the child will be more likely to use these conversations to solve problems with friends.

Inviting the Child to Talk

To invite the child to talk, encourage them without communicating any of your own feelings or judgments. You can do this in two ways:

By a noncommittal expression of interest:
- Really.
- You did?
- That's interesting.

or:

You can use a more explicit invitation to talk:
- Tell me about it.
- Let's talk about it.
- Go ahead, I'm listening.

These invitations keep the conversational ball with the child. They encourage children to continue talking about their own feelings, thoughts, and opinions. Other comments could grab the conversational ball away from the child: asking questions, giving advice, and teaching or moralizing introduce your own ideas and feelings into the conversation. These comments tell children what they're expected to think and feel, and may put a damper on their saying anything different.

Keeping the Child Talking

To listen well, parents need to abandon any attempts to react to or evaluate what their child is saying. The listening parent's job is to serve as a conversational "mirror" to the child. Think about the essential meaning of what the child is saying. Pick out the words that seem most important to the child, feelings that seem most compelling, or ideas the child repeats more than once. Reflect the child's ideas by repeating those essential statements back to them. To avoid monopolizing the conversation, keep these reflections to a single sentence.

Good listening improves the relationship between the parent and child. The experience of being heard and understood is very satisfying, and the child is more likely to seek the parent out for similar discussions in the future. Moreover, once the parent has listened well to the child, the child is more likely to listen in return. Being listened to helps the child feel appreciated and important.

Good listening also helps children solve their own problems. When children hear their own ideas reflected back to them, they are likely to begin analyzing their problem on their own. Thinking can proceed more clearly when the child can give attention to what really happened, instead of what parents will think. By listening well, the parent can become a "sounding board" for the child.

Good listening also helps children find out how they're feeling. After listening to themselves talk through a problem, children hear the feelings in their own words. Moreover, when parents listen well, the children are allowed to see and accept unpleasant or negative feelings. They are likely to see all sides of the problem more accurately.

Listening in this way will feel awkward at first, and many children may comment that you're "talking funny." Still with practice, good listening will become second nature, and you will have a natural way to respond to the friendship problems that come home with your child.

Here is an example of active listening:

Christine: Two second graders are bothering me a lot at recess, and I can't get them to stop.

Father: I can see that it's bothering you a lot.

Christine: Yeah, and I can't get any of the teachers to believe me; they think it's not really happening.

Father: You've tried talking to the teachers, and that's not working.

Christine: They don't believe me. They tell me not to worry about it.

Father: And you're still worried.

Christine: Maybe I'll tell Mrs. Stevenson. Those kids are in her class. She'll make them stop.

Father: Telling the other teachers didn't work, but you think that telling Mrs. Stevenson might work.

Christine: Well, they're in Mrs. Stevenson's class. And sometimes she listens. But sometimes she doesn't. I don't think teachers like you talking like that on the playground.

Father: They don't like you talking like that.

Christine: They don't like you telling. They always say, "Take care of it yourself."

Father: And you're not sure you can take care of it yourself.

Christine: They call me "ET's wife." I could call them corn-
         heads. They wouldn't like that.
Father: So now you think you can handle it.
Christine: I might get in trouble.
Father: You might get in trouble, but sometimes it's worth it.
Christine: Yeah.

DISCUSSION QUESTIONS

1. Think about the last time you talked with your child
   about friends and friendships. Who started the conversation? What did you try to do to help? Was your child
   able to act on the conversation?
2. Remember the "talking times" you've had with your
   child. At what time of day did they usually occur?
   Where were you when you were talking? At what time
   and place are your child's "talking times"?
3. Think about the last time you talked with a friend
   about a problem. What did they do to try to help you?
   Did it work?

TOPIC 2 ACTIVITY: REACT TO CHILD STATEMENTS

Imagine that your child has just walked in the door from school
or the neighborhood park. As the door is flung open he or she calls
out one of the statements on the left. In the right-hand column,
write a "good listening" response you could make in return:

"I can't stand my teacher. She's such   _____
a grouch; she yells at me all the time.   _____
She sent me to the office again today—   _____
I can never do anything right."   _____

"How come I can't go to the mall with   _____
Sarah? Her mom always lets her go!   _____
You never let me do anything!"   _____
                                               _____

"I can't stand Joey! He's a jerk!"   _____
                                               _____
                                               _____
                                               _____

"Katie called me a klutz on the playground   _____
again today. All the kids laughed at me."   _____
                                                           _____
                                                           _____

"The teacher yelled at me for not getting   _____
my assignment done in class, but I just   _____
don't get it! I can't help it if I'm not   _____
as smart as the other kids in my class."   _____

"I'm always the last one to get picked for   _____
the kickball team. No one ever wants me   _____
on their team."   _____

"It wasn't my fault that Kevin and I got   _____
into a fight! He started it—it's his   _____
fault! How come I always get blamed?"   _____

"I don't know what's wrong with me.   _____
Jenny used to like me, but now she doesn't.   _____
She never comes over here to play anymore.   _____
And if I go to her house she's always   _____
playing with Stacey, and the two of them   _____
play together and have fun, and I just   _____
stand there all by myself."   _____

"I hate school! The kids and the teacher   _____
are always picking on me! I'm never   _____
going back!"   _____

"Jenny and I had so much fun at recess   _____
today! We played jump rope and hopscotch   _____
and kickball! She's my best friend!"   _____
                                                           _____

"Guess what, Mom? I made the soccer team!"   _____
                                                           _____
                                                           _____
                                                           _____

TOPIC 3: SETTING GOALS SYSTEMATICALLY

Goal setting is a commonsense strategy used to help children understand how to gain control over their relationships with friends. Children are helped to set daily goals for their own social behavior, to evaluate their progress toward those goals, and to follow up on the evaluation with revised goals.

Personal habits are very difficult to change for many reasons:

We don't always notice or pay attention to our own habitual ways of behaving.

We practice our habits almost automatically without making any effort to control the behavior.

We grow accustomed to the routine provided by our own habits.

For these reasons, changing habitual behaviors can only be accomplished with patience and finesse.

The same is true with children. Some of the problematic social behaviors they use have become personal habits. Although it is easy for adults to see the need for a child to behave differently with friends, and easy for adults to suggest simple but effective changes in friendship practices, getting the child to actually change these behaviors is very difficult. Goal setting is one way to help the child make effective changes in friendship behavior.

To set goals for improving children's friendships, first observe how the child is behaving now with friends. To be truly helpful, it is necessary to keep a written record of your observations.

After observing what your child is doing now with friends, think about what he or she could be doing differently. Some of your ideas will come from your own friendship experiences, and others can come from the discussions in these parent meetings.

Now you're ready to begin setting goals with your child. Some rules for effective goal setting include the following:

1. *Choose a goal that your child has control over.* The goal "I'll play with Jean after school" may present a problem if Jean chooses not to play. A better goal would be "I'll ask Jean to play after school," because that is something your child can indeed accomplish independently.
2. *Choose a goal that tells your child what to do rather than what not to do.* The goal "I'll stop and count to 10

when I get angry at a friend" is better than "I won't yell at friends." Although the second goal may be important, it doesn't give the child any directions about what to do instead, and so will be less helpful.

3. *Choose goals that your child will probably be successful in meeting.* For a child who stands alone every recess, the goal "I will play with a friend during recess" is probably impossible. A better goal would be "I will ask a friend to play with me during one recess period." To plan for success, break big goals down into very small steps, and help your child attempt them one step at a time.

4. *Hook your child into the goal-setting process by keeping early goals easy enough to ensure success.* Most frequently, the first goals set with children should require them to do things they have already done successfully. Later goals can require that they begin to practice new skills in very small steps. In this way, by the time the children attempt the more difficult goals, they will expect themselves to be able to accomplish them.

5. *Make goals specific enough for the child to follow without confusion or indecision.* Rather than the goal "I will follow the rules of the game when playing," set the goal "I will wait for my turn when playing Rummy with Michael." Because the second goal is more specific, it provides your child with more guidance about exactly what to do and when. As another example, setting a goal like "I will ask Jamie to play kickball at recess" will give you an opportunity to help your child decide who will be a good classmate to ask to play, what would be a good game to play, and when would be a good time to ask.

6. *Ensure better participation in the goal-setting process by getting your child to set the goals with you.* Goals you set for children without their input are more likely to be ignored or rejected by them.

7. *Keep careful records of the goals you set and the results of each goal.* Then periodically review your records with your child so that they can see the progress they've made. Looking at records of goals set in past weeks, and noting that those early behaviors are now easy and successful, gives your child the message "You can change how you act and help yourself make friends."

Possible Goals to Set for Children With Few Friends

Goals that encourage a child to do something with a friend:

Watch to find out what things a friend likes to do.
Ask a friend to do something together.
Say yes to a friend who asks to do something together.
Play something with a friend even if you don't want to.
Learn to play something new because friends like to.
Play with a friend for longer periods of time.
Ask a group of friends if you can play too.

Think of another one _____

Goals that encourage a child to be helpful and cooperative:

Follow the rules for a game.
Allow a friend to choose the game you play.
Take turns with friends.
Let a friend take the first turn.
Help a friend with a job they have to do.
Do something you don't want to because a friend wants to.

Think of another one _____

Goals that encourage a child to be friendly:

Smile at a friend when you see him or her.
Say something nice to a friend.
Tell a friend something you like about them.
Use a nice voice when talking to friends.
Think of a favor you could do for a friend, and do it.
Notice when a friend is unhappy.
Ask a friend if you can do something to help.

Think of another one _____

TOPIC 3 ACTIVITY: SETTING A GOOD GOAL FOR YOUR OWN CHILD

Pick one goal that would be good for your child:

_____

Now, think about what your child will have to know about to meet that goal. Will they have to understand something new about friends or understand friendship in a different way?

_____

Are there any new skills your child may have to learn to meet that goal?

_____

_____

Now use your thoughts about what your child will have to know, or skills your child may have to learn, to rewrite the goal you started out with.

_____

Think about steps your child will have to take to meet that goal.

Step 1: _____

Step 2: _____

Step 3: _____

Step 4: _____

Mark whether you expect these steps to be easy or difficult for your child.

Review these steps, and your thoughts about what your child's skills are, and decide whether you should choose just one step as your goal. If you decide to do that, rewrite the goal one more time.

_____

_____

_____

Discuss your goal with the group, and decide with them whether it satisfies the rules for good goal setting. Is it:

A goal your child has control over?	☐ Yes	☐ No
A goal that tells your child what to do, rather than what not to do?	☐ Yes	☐ No
A goal that your child will probably be successful in meeting?	☐ Yes	☐ No
Specific enough that your child will know exactly what to do to meet it?	☐ Yes	☐ No

TOPIC 4: HELPING CHILDREN SOLVE FRIENDSHIP PROBLEMS

Children often seem "trapped" by the difficulties they're having with friends. They become caught in a pattern of inaction because they're not sure what they *can* do, or because they can't make up their mind. When children seem particularly confused, they'll often ask, "What *should* I do?" or "What would you do?"

Think of a time when you've tried to answer that question. More times than not, when a parent makes a suggestion, the child will answer either "I did that already" or "That won't work." When you stop to think about it, even if a plan of action is obvious to you, it isn't necessarily obvious to your child. The two of you think differently about friendships and friendship problems. So it's not surprising that the wisdom of your suggestions won't always be recognized by your child.

An alternative to telling a child what to do is helping them make their own plan. Left to themselves, many children can't think systematically enough about friendship problems to develop an appropriate plan. However, when the planning is broken down into smaller problem-solving steps, children can develop plans of action that fit their understanding of problems and fit their understanding of themselves.

Step 1: What Is the Problem?

This first step is often skipped because the problem seems apparent to adults. In many cases, however, children can misperceive the problem and so be unable to develop a good solution. Consider the example of a new child standing on the edge of a game of tag. We may understand the problem as "How to help the new kid join the game," whereas our child may see the problem as "How to get that kid out of the way." The first step in any problem-solving plan is to agree together on what the problem is. Ask your child to describe it to you, and if the description surprises you, talk about it together.

Step 2: Describe at Least Three Different Things You Could Do

Thinking of only one possible solution is a second mistake many children make in solving problems. When you ask children to think of many different ways to solve a problem, their best ideas don't always come first. Systematically solving problems requires that children spend enough time thinking of solutions to develop their high-quality ideas.

Be careful to not evaluate any of the suggestions when thinking of possible solutions. Don't allow your child to evaluate the suggestions either. Evaluation often stops a person's flow of thought. Commenting on the ideas, even when positive, encourages your child to think of ideas that you'll like rather than to think of many different ideas. If your child begins to comment on any of the ideas or to reject them at this point, interrupt and say, "We'll talk about whether the idea is good or bad in a few minutes."

Step 3: Describe the Consequences of Each Idea

Remember that we want children to choose the best idea—the one that will lead to better friendships. With effort, most children can describe what will happen if they use one of their ideas, but they may not stop to think about it. Before allowing them to choose any of their ideas, ask them to describe a consequence for each of the three ideas. If their descriptions are unrealistic, ask them to act out the idea with you. Sometimes children can understand in action what they cannot understand in words.

Step 4: Choosing an Idea

Once your child has identified the problem, thought of several different solutions to try, and described possible consequences of each solution, allow your child to choose the idea to use. Children may not always choose the best idea; parents can become discouraged at this point if their careful guidance hasn't led the child to an obviously best solution. Remember that the goal is to have children make deliberate plans to solve their problems with friends. They are much more likely to implement a plan that they chose themselves, and are likely to learn as much from a bad plan as they could from a good one.

Step 5: Charting a Course of Action

Being able to describe a plan in words doesn't always mean that the child can actually do it. Before closing down the planning session, check to see exactly how the child will follow through with the plan. For example, if a child has decided to ignore the teasing of another child, pretend to be the other child and ask your child to practice ignoring you. Or if your child has decided to ask a friend over to play, pretend to be the friend and have your child practice the invitation first.

Step 6: Check Back

Remember that the plan is your child's responsibility. Don't give him or her extra reminders to follow it, and don't offer to help. Do check back in a few days to see how it went. Help your child feel proud if the plan worked; if it didn't work, talk about what to do instead. Being unsuccessful hurts most if you begin to believe you can't be anything else.

DISCUSSION QUESTIONS

1. Think of a recent time when your child talked to you about a problem. Did your child decide to do anything different about the problem? Whose idea was the solution? Did your child actually carry out the plan? Did it work? What would you do about the problem now?

2. Think of a time when you solved a problem for your child. You may have spoken to your child's teacher, called the mother of one of their friends, or made up a new rule that would change the way your child was behaving. Did your solution work? Was there anything that your child could have done instead to have solved the problem? What would you do about the problem now?

TOPIC 4 ACTIVITY: HELPING YOUR CHILD UNDERSTAND FRIENDSHIP PROBLEMS

Read the following descriptions of friendship problems. For each problem, think about (a) how your child would describe the problem, and (b) what solutions your child might think of. (Remember that the objective is to *help your child* think of alternative solutions, and not to tell him or her what he or she should do!)

1. Your child walks home each day with two neighbor children. Because they're a year older, they make your child walk several steps behind. How would your child describe the problem?

   _____

   _____

   _____

   _____

What are some solutions your child might think of?

_____

_____

_____

_____

2. A new child moves into your neighborhood. When you invite the new child to your house to play, your child's "best friend" becomes angry, claiming, "You can't be both our friends. You're not my friend anymore." How would your child describe the problem?

_____

_____

_____

_____

What are some solutions your child might think of?

_____

_____

_____

_____

3. A class is asked to write a story about the "worst day in your life." Two girls sitting at your child's table write about a fight they had the year before, and as they remember it, they become angry once more. How would your child describe the problem?

_____

_____

_____

_____

What are some solutions your child might think of?

_____

_____

_____

_____

4. The teacher asks your child to be "in charge" of the class while he steps out of the room. Four children begin to throw books once the teacher leaves the room, and your child writes their names on the board. Now the whole class is angry and refuses to play with your child. How would your child describe the problem?

_____

_____

_____

_____

What are some solutions your child might think of?

_____

_____

_____

_____

TOPIC 5: CHILDREN'S ABILITY
TO UNDERSTAND THE OTHER CHILD

Social learning is different from other kinds of learning. For one thing, social learning occurs almost accidentally. Children learn about social rules and social behavior through experience and exploration. Through trial and error, they try out new ways of behaving with friends. They discover which behaviors work, and which ones don't. Without childhood friendships, children have no "experiments" with which to practice social skills.

Social learning is also different because it's not always clear what is being learned. There are definite rules for how we should behave with other people; the problem is that these are frequently unspoken rules that everyone knows about but no one talks about. Children learn these rules in somewhat arbitrary ways—by watching other people make social mistakes or making mistakes themselves, or by watching other people who are socially graceful and trying to imitate those graces themselves. Children aren't usually given many helpful directions for social behavior. Adults don't usually tell a child, "When you want to play with a group of kids, go up and watch them play for a while. Then, if they don't notice you, ask if you can join. Be sure to pick a good time to ask when you won't interrupt the game."

Adults don't explain social rules to children because they don't always realize that the rules exist until after they're broken. One child, Jamie, was told repeatedly that all he had to do to join the lunchtime baseball team was to ask. So finally he did. He walked up and asked the batter while the pitcher threw the last strike. We hadn't thought to tell him not to interrupt the game.

Because social learning occurs through observation and practice, it is less predictable than other kinds of learning. Social interactions don't always happen the same way. It's difficult to practice social rules if the behavior of the other person isn't always consistent. Christine may be on her best behavior on Saturday morning when she asks Jenny to play, but if Jenny's just been arguing with her mom about breakfast, she may snap crossly at Christine. Social rules also differ depending on the child's relationship within a group. For example, one child may be allowed to tease another child as a joke, but a different child could be angrily shunned for teasing in the same way.

Adults aren't usually surprised when another person's social behaviors don't follow the rules because adults can usually explain what happened. If Christine complained to her teacher, she might be told, "Jenny's probably having a bad day." A child who got in trouble for teasing might be told, "But you didn't say it the same way." Adults aren't surprised because they can use their vast social experience to "read" the other person. Children's social skills also improve greatly as they develop the ability to "read" others. They do this by figuring out the other child's moods, intentions, thoughts, personal characteristics, and perceptions. This ability to read other people allows them to adjust the way they behave to that person in that situation.

Developmental psychologists call this ability *role taking* or *perspective taking*. Role taking is the ability to take the position of the other person and to understand that person's perspective. It is an important skill that one person uses to understand the other person.

There are five ways that a child can understand another person. Each of these is a slightly different way of understanding, and each develops gradually as a child grows older. Table AH.1 summarizes the development of role taking.

1. *Understanding what another person sees*: The ability to understand what another person might see is recognizing that the same physical object looks different when viewed from a different angle. For example, an object placed between two people will look different depending upon the particular view each has.

   There are three developmental stages that children go through in learning about differing visual perspectives. Between the ages of 4 and 6, children are unable to recognize that the visual perspective of another differs from one's own. At approximately 6 or 7 years of age, they begin to understand that perspectives differ, but will usually be mistaken when trying to describe these differences. Finally, between the ages of 7 and 9, children are able to clearly and accurately describe differences in perspective.

2. *Understanding how another person feels*: The ability to understand how another person feels is described as empathy. Empathy is attempting to feel the emotions of another person. It is considered an important cause of kindness in both children and adults.

   By the age of 3, children can recognize that certain familiar situations typically bring about certain emotions, such as happiness or fear. At the preschool ages, children are better able to identify another's feelings if they are familiar with the situation of the other, and if the other person is similar to themselves. By approximately 6 to 7½ years of age, children respond to questions about feelings of others, but identify only global states such as happy, sad, angry, or afraid.

By approximately ages 7½ to 9, children identify emotions more specifically, and include references to more complex feelings such as jealous, worried, upset, and nervous. Finally, by approximately age 12 and older, references are made to more specific emotions, and children also become able to discuss the thoughts and intentions of others.

3. *Understanding what the other thinks*: The ability to understand what another thinks is related to one's understanding of what they see and how they feel. By the age of 6, children are capable of realizing that others have thoughts that are different from their own. However, it is not until the age of 10 or 11 that children understand that these different thoughts can occur at the same time. At this age, children realize that they can take another's perspective at the same time that the other is taking their perspective. *Mutual role taking* involves respecting each other's different perspectives as equally credible.

4. *Understanding what the intentions of others are*: By the age of 4, a child begins to make judgments about acts that are performed intentionally, as compared to those that are accidental. For example, they're likely to forgive a child who bumps into them by accident. By the age of 6, children are generally able to take intentions into account with a high degree of accuracy. However, if extreme damage occurs as the result of an accident (e.g., Mom's favorite vase is broken), a child at this age may ignore its accidental nature and recommend severe punishment. Significant developmental changes occur between the ages of 6 and 9. Children are able to judge the causes of behavior more accurately. They begin to interpret others' behaviors more accurately, and they realize that accidents do not necessitate placing blame.

5. *Understanding what the other person is like*: Understanding what another person is like is often termed *person perception*. With development, children make increasing differentiations among people. Young children focus on the external qualities of others (such as

appearance), but older children are able to focus on internal qualities such as values and beliefs.

DISCUSSION QUESTIONS

1. Think about the following common games that your child plays with other kids or typical conversations they have. What "role-taking" skills do they need to use in those situations (Battleship, Candyland, football or soccer, hide-and-seek, card games, Authors, or Fish)?
2. How well do you see your child taking the perspective of the other? Given your child's age, is this appropriate?
3. How does your child describe friends to you? What qualities or characteristics seem most important to your child? How accurately does your child describe others' behaviors and feelings?

Table AH.1   Development of Children's Ability to Take the Perspective of Another

	Understanding What the Other Might See	Understanding How the Other Might Feel	Understanding What the Other Thinks	Understanding the Intentions of the Other
Ages 4–6	Doesn't know that what the other sees differs from oneself	Can recognize expected feelings in familiar situations		Beginning to judge acts performed intentionally differently from accidental ones
Ages 6–7	Knows that what the other sees differs, but can't describe how	Can answer questions of how others feel using global words like *happy* or *sad*	Realizes that others have thoughts that are different from their own	Reliably takes intentions into account when judging behavior unless damage is extreme
Ages 7–12	Differences in what the other sees can be described accurately	Can use more specific feeling words like *upset, nervous,* or *jealous*	Can describe what others are thinking with some accuracy	Can coordinate information about several causes when judging behavior
Ages 12 and up		Uses even more specific feeling words, and links these to the intentions of the other	Realizes that others are trying to guess their thoughts at the same time as they try to guess others	Realizes that others are figuring out their own intentions at the same time as they try to guess others' intentions

TOPIC 5 ACTIVITY: CHILDREN'S ROLE-TAKING QUESTIONNAIRE

Think about the following situations. Some may be familiar to your child; others may not. Predict what your child might do in each of these.

1. After an art activity, your son volunteered to stay after school to help his teacher straighten the classroom. While the teacher was out of the room, your son noticed some papers on the floor under a classmate's desk. Just as he picked them up and opened the desk to replace them, his classmate entered the room and immediately accused your son of "snooping in his desk and trying to copy his work." In this situation, how well would your child understand differences in what the other child was seeing?

___ Very well
___ Somewhat well
___ Not very well
___ Not at all well

Has your child been in situations like this one or in similar situations? How did your child respond?

_____

_____

_____

_____

2. At recess, a group of children played a game of softball. Two captains were assigned to pick teams. As always, the last person to be chosen was the same overweight, awkward child. A group of teammates moaned when they got "stuck" with him, and the captain assigned him to play far right field because the ball is never hit there. In this situation, how well would your child understand how this child is feeling?

___ Very well
___ Somewhat well
___ Not very well
___ Not at all well

Has your child been in situations where another child was being teased or in similar situations? What did he or she do?

_____

_____

_____

_____

3. One of your daughter's best neighborhood friends is a year older and one grade ahead of her. Although they still walk to school together, once they get there your daughter is quickly abandoned as her friend rushes to join her classmates. Even on weekends, the neighbor prefers to go to others' homes or to the mall with her other friends. In this situation, how well would your child understand why the neighbor is behaving this way?

___ Very well
___ Somewhat well
___ Not very well
___ Not at all well

Has your child been in situations like this one or in similar situations? What did he or she do?

_____

_____

_____

_____

4. Your child has invited a new classmate over to play on your home computer. Although your child has become very knowledgeable about computers and uses "computer jargon" very well, the classmate is completely inexperienced with computers. Your child is excited about a complex new computer game and must explain the game to the friend. In this situation, how well would your child understand that his or her peer may think differently about computers than he or she does?

___ Very well
___ Somewhat well
___ Not very well
___ Not at all well

Has your child been in situations like this one or in similar situations? What did your child do?

_____

_____

_____

_____

5. Your daughter is a good student and a hard worker. Although she has some friends, she is generally a quiet, reserved child. There is a group of children in her class who are known to be "lazy," with irresponsible work habits and study skills. One of these children has recently begun approaching your daughter at school, asking her to work "together" on some math assignments. In this situation, how well would your child understand the personal characteristics of his or her classmate?

___ Very well
___ Somewhat well
___ Not very well
___ Not at all well

Has your child been in situations like this one or in similar situations? What did he or she do?

_____

_____

_____

_____

TOPIC 6: HELPING YOUR CHILD SEE
THE OTHER POINT OF VIEW

To fully understand how another child feels when something happens, a child must be (a) sensitive to the other person's feelings and problems, (b) able to think about different ways of acting, (c) able to think about different ways to solve a problem, and (d) sensitive to the consequences of his or her own behaviors.

As parents, you are in good position to encourage alternative ways of thinking about others. Role taking, or helping your child understand the thoughts, behaviors, feelings, and different views of other children, is a skill that can be enhanced through careful listening and discussion. To encourage role taking in your children:

1. Provide opportunities for your child to identify his or her own feelings and the feelings of others in different situations (for example, distressed, fearful, or worried). Help your child label the other child's feelings, especially when he or she is unable to understand what has happened. It's easier for children to talk about a situation that has just happened and harder for them to talk about made-up or make-believe situations.
2. Encourage your child to imagine himself or herself in the place of another. Point out the similarities and differences between your child and other children.
3. Ask your child to consider the result of what he or she does on others, or how his or her actions will make others feel. Give labels to the feelings of the other child. (For example, "After you yelled at Johnny, he looked very sad.")

To communicate actively and encourage role taking with your child, it is important to provide an opportunity for talk. Spend several minutes actively listening to your child. Once the story seems complete, use one of the following to invite your child to consider how the other child felt or what he or she was thinking:

I'm wondering what Jenny was thinking then.

Try for a few minutes to pretend that you were Jason. What do you think he was feeling?

Let's think about Mike now. If you were Mike, what would you feel like?

Something must have been going through Erin's mind then. What do you think it was?

If you were Tina, what would you be thinking about then?

I'm trying to decide what John was thinking in his mind when that happened.

What would you have felt like to be Brian then?

The following is an example of a dialogue to encourage role taking:

Mother: Jason, you were yelling at Nathan in the backyard, and now you look angry.

Jason: Nathan hit me with a branch off the tree.

Mother: With a branch...

Jason: Nathan's always doing things like that. He just picks it up and hits me.

Mother: He hits you for no reason.

Jason: Yeah. He was playing soldier and swinging the stick all around, and then he hit me in the face. He should be more careful. He knows that he could hurt my eyes.

Mother: So it makes you angry that he wasn't more careful.

Jason: Yeah.

Mother: And then you yelled at him and told him to go home.

Jason: Yeah.

Mother: Well let's pretend you're Nathan. You're playing soldier and all of a sudden the stick hits a friend in the face. What are you thinking when you watch the stick hit him?

Jason: I don't know. Nathan had the stick.

Mother: But now we're pretending you're Nathan. What are you thinking when you watch the stick hit a friend?

Jason: I don't know.... "Uh-oh, I'm in big trouble now."

Mother: So Nathan probably knew when the stick hit you that you were going to be getting mad.

Jason: Yeah.

Mother: And then you were yelling at him.... What was he thinking then?

Jason: Probably.... "I knew it. I knew I was in trouble."

Mother: What do you suppose he's thinking now?

DISCUSSION QUESTIONS

1. Think about the last time you talked to your child about a problem that he or she was having with friends. What was the problem? What did *you* say or do to help with the problem? How was the problem resolved?

2. Think about a time when you were watching a sad television program or movie with your child. What aspects of the program did you discuss? Was your child able to identify "sadness" as a major theme of the movie? Could your child understand why different characters in the movie were feeling sad?

TOPIC 6 ACTIVITY: WAYS TO PROMPT ROLE TAKING

Think about the situations described earlier. Decide what you could say to your child in each situation to help him or her think of the other child.

1. After an art activity, your son volunteered to stay after school to help his teacher straighten the classroom. While the teacher was out of the room, your son noticed some papers on the floor under a classmate's desk. Just as he picked them up and opened the desk to replace them, his classmate entered the room and immediately accused your son of "snooping in his desk and trying to copy his work." Your son came home after school very upset. He says, "Mike always says I did things, and then I get into trouble." What would you say to your child in this situation? How would you help him see the other child's view?

   _____

   _____

   _____

   _____

2. At recess today, a group of children played a group game of softball. Two captains were assigned to pick teams. As always, the last person to be chosen was the same overweight, awkward child. A group of

teammates moaned when they got "stuck" with him, and the captain assigned him to play far right field because the ball is never hit there. Your daughter came home very upset. She says, "They always do that to TJ. He looks awful when they tease him like that." What would you say to your child in this situation? How would you help her see the other's view?

_____

_____

_____

_____

3. One of your daughter's best neighborhood friends is a year older and one grade ahead of her. Although they still walk to school together, once they get there your daughter is quickly abandoned as her friend rushes to join her classmates. Even on weekends, the neighbor prefers to go to others' homes or to the mall with her other friends. Your daughter is very upset. She tells you, "No one likes me anymore. I don't have a single friend left." What would you say to your child in this situation? How would you help her see the other child's view?

_____

_____

_____

_____

4. Your child has invited a new classmate over to play on your home computer. Although your child has become very knowledgeable about computers and uses "computer jargon" very well, the classmate is completely inexperienced with computers. Your child is excited about a complex new computer game and must explain the game to his peer. After the friend left, your child told you, "Jamie's a dummy. He's never any fun. I don't want him here again." What would you say to your child in this situation? How would you help him see the other child's view?

_____

_____

_____

_____

5. Your daughter is a good student and a hard worker.
Although she has some friends, she is generally a quiet,
reserved child. There is a group of children in her
class who are known to be "lazy," with irresponsible
work habits and study skills. One of these children has
recently begun approaching your daughter at school,
asking her to work "together" on some math assignments. Your daughter feels uncomfortable about this,
but wants to be liked by the group. She says, "I want
to work with him, but sometimes it doesn't seem fair."
What would you say to your child in this situation?
How would you help her see the other child's view?

_____

_____

_____

_____

References

Ainsworth, M. D. S. (1989). Attachments beyond infancy. *American Psychologist, 44,* 709–716.

Ainsworth, M. D. S., & Bowlby, J. (1991). An ethological approach to personality development. *American Psychologist, 46,* 331–341.

Asher, S. R., & Coie, J. D. (1990). *Peer rejection in childhood.* New York: Cambridge University Press.

Asher, S. R., Parker, J. G., & Walker, D. L. (1996). Distinguishing friendship from acceptance: Implications for intervention and assessment. In W. M. Bukowski, A. F. Newcomb, & W. W. Hartup (Eds.), *The company they keep: Friendship in childhood and adolescence* (pp. 366–405). New York: Cambridge University Press.

Bandura, A. (1977). *Social learning theory.* Englewood Cliffs, NJ: Prentice Hall.

Barclay, J. R. (1992). Sociometry, temperament, and school psychology. In T. R. Kratochwill, S. N. Elliott, & M. Gettinger (Eds.), *Advances in school psychology* (3rd ed., Chap. 3). Hillsdale, NJ: Erlbaum.

Barlow, D. H., Nock, M. K., & Hersen, M. (2008). *Single case experimental designs: Strategies for studying behavior change* (3rd ed.). Columbus, OH: Allyn & Bacon.

Batsche, G. M., & Porter, L. J. (2006). Bullying. In G. C. Bear & K. M. Minke (Eds.), *Children's needs III: Development, prevention and intervention* (pp. 135–148). Bethesda, MD: National Association of School Psychologists.

Baumrind, D. (1989). Rearing competent children. In W. Damon (Ed.), *Child development today and tomorrow* (pp. 349–378). San Francisco: Jossey Bass.

Bay-Hinitz, A. K., Peterson, R. F., & Quilitch, H. R. (1994). Cooperative games: A way to modify aggressive and cooperative behaviors in young children. *Journal of Applied Behavioral Analysis, 27,* 435–446.

Bear, G. G., Cavalier, A. R., & Manning, M. A. (2005). *Developing self-discipline and preventing and correcting misbehavior.* Boston: Pearson Education.

Beckwith, J. (2003). The challenging playground: How the law of unintended consequences has diminished children's play. *Landscape Architecture Specific News, 19,* 78–82.

Bernstein, B. (1972). Social class, language, and socialization. In P. Giglioli (Ed.), *Language and social context* (pp. 157–178). Harmondsworth, UK: Penguin.

Blatchford, P. (1996). "We did more then": Changes in pupils' perceptions of breaktime (recess) from 7 to 16 years. *Journal of Research in Childhood Education, 11*, 14–24.

Blatchford, P. (1999). Friendships at school: The role of break-times. *Education 3–13, 27*, 60–65.

Blatchford, P., Baines, E., & Pellegrini, A. (2003). The social context of school playground games: Sex and ethnic differences and changes over time after entry to junior school. *British Journal of Developmental Psychology, 21*, 481–505.

Boulton, M., & Smith, P. K. (1993). Ethnic, gender partner, and activity preferences in mixed race children's social competence. In C. Hart (Ed.), *Children on playgrounds* (pp. 210–238). Albany: State University of New York Press.

Bowlby, J. (1969). *Attachment and loss.* New York: Basic Books.

Butcher, D. A. (1999). Enhancing social skills through school social work interventions during recess: Gender differences. *Social Work in Education, 21*, 249–262.

Calo, K., & Ingram, P. (1994). *Playground leaders* (No. ED 376 984). Wells, ME: Maine Center for Educational Services.

Chauvet, M. J., & Blatchford, P. (1993). Group composition and national curriculum assessment at 7 years. *Educational Research, 35*, 189–196.

Chuoke, M., & Eyman, B. (1997). Play fair—and not just at recess. *Educational Leadership, 54*, 53–55.

Clements, R. L. (Ed.). (2000). *Elementary school recess: Selected readings, games, and activities for teachers and parents.* Boston: American Press.

Corsaro, W. A. (2003). *We're friends, right? Inside kids' culture.* Washington, DC: Joseph Henry.

Crick, N., & Gropeter, J. (1995). Relational aggression, gender, and social psychological adjustment. *Child Development, 66*, 710–722.

Crone, D. A., Horner, R. H., & Hawken, L. S. (2004). *Responding to problem behavior in schools: The Behavior Education Program.* New York: Guilford.

Developmental Studies Center. (1996). *Ways we want our class to be: Class meetings that build commitment to kindness and learning.* Oakland, CA: Author.

Dodge, K. A. (1983). Behavioral antecedents of peer social status. *Child Development, 54*, 1386–1399.

Doll, B. (1996). Children without friends: Implications for practice and policy. *School Psychology Review, 25*, 165–183.

Doll, B. (2008, August). Ecological approaches to creating classrooms that promote success. Paper presented at the 116th convention of the American Psychological Association, Boston.

Doll, B., Kurien, S., LeClair, C., Spies, R., Champion, A., & Osborn, A. (2009). The ClassMaps Survey: A framework for promoting positive classroom environments. In R. Gilman, S. Huebner, & M. Furlong (Eds.), *Handbook of positive psychology in the schools* (pp. 213–227). New York: Routledge.

Doll, B., LeClair, C., & Kurien, S. (2009). Effective classrooms: Classroom learning environments that foster school success (pp. 791–807). In T. Gutkin & C. Reynolds (Eds.), *The handbook of school psychology*. Hoboken, NJ: John Wiley.

Doll, B., Murphy, P., & Song, S. (2003). The relationship between children's self-reported recess problems, and peer acceptance and friendships. *Journal of School Psychology, 41*, 113–130.

Doll, B., Zucker, S., & Brehm, K. (2004). *Resilient classrooms: Creating healthy environments for learning*. New York: Guilford.

Dwyer, K., & Osher, D. (2000). *Safeguarding our children: An action guide*. Washington, DC: U.S. Departments of Education and Justice, American Institutes for Research.

Eisenberg, N., & Mussen, P. H. (1989). *The roots of prosocial behavior in children*. New York: Cambridge University Press.

Espelage, D. L., & Swearer, S. M. (2003). Research on school bullying and victimization: What have we learned and where do we go from here? *School Psychology Review, 32*, 365–383.

Gabarino, J. (2003). *See Jane hit: Why girls are growing more violent and what we can do about it*. New York: Penguin.

GamesKidsPlay.net. (n.d.). *Welcome to GamesKidsPlay.net*. Retrieved August 5, 2009 from http://www.gameskids play.net

Gettinger, M., Doll, B., & Salmon, D. (1994). Effects of social problem-solving, goal-setting, and parent training on children's peer relations. *Journal of Applied Developmental Psychology, 15*, 141–163.

Greenberg, M. T., Kusche, C. A., Mihalic, S. F., & Elliott, D. S. (1998). Promoting alternative thinking strategies. In D. S. Elliot, (Ed.), *Blueprints for violence prevention.* Denver, CO: C&M Press.

Hartup, W. W. (1996). The company they keep: Friendships and their developmental significance. *Child Development, 67,* 1–13.

High, B. (2008). *Bully police USA: Does your state have an anti-bully law?* Retrieved December 23, 2008, from http://www.bullypolice.org

Humphreys, A., & Smith, P. K. (1984). Rough-and-tumble in preschool and playground. In P. K. Smith (Ed.), *Play in animals and humans* (pp. 241–270). London: Blackwell.

Ladd, G. W. (2005). *Children's peer relations and social competence: A century of progress.* New Haven, CT: Yale University Press.

LaRusso, M. D., Brown, J. L., Jones, S. M., & Aber, J. L. (2008, April). School climate, relationships, and behavior in elementary school: Longitudinal and mixed method analyses. Paper presented at the annual convention of the American Educational Research Association, Chicago.

Lefevre, D. N. (2002). *Best new games: 77 games and 7 trust activities for all ages and abilities.* Champaign, IL: Human Kinetics.

Leff, S. S., Costigan, T., & Power, T. J. (2004). Using participatory research to develop a playground-based prevention program. *Journal of School Psychology, 42,* 3–21.

Leff, S. S., Kupersmidt, J. B, Patterson, C., & Power, T. J. (1999). Factors influencing teacher predictions of peer bullying and victimization. *School Psychology Review, 28,* 505–517.

Leff, S. S., Power, T. J., Manz, P. H., Costigan, T. E., & Nabors, L. A. (2001). School-based aggression prevention programs for young children: Current status and implications for violence prevention. *School Psychology Review, 30,* 343–360.

Lewis, T., Colvin, G., & Sugai, G. (2000). The effects of precorrection and active supervision on the recess behavior of elementary students. *Education and Treatment of Children, 23,* 109–121.

Lewis, T. E., & Phillipsen, L. C. (1998). Interactions on an elementary school playground: Variations by age, gender, race, group size, and playground area. *Child Study Journal, 28,* 309–321.

Lewis, T., Powers, L. J., Kelk, M. J., & Newcomer, L. L. (2002). Reducing problem behaviors on the playground: An investigation of the application of school-wide positive behavior supports. *Psychology in the Schools, 39,* 181–190.

Lewis, T. J., Sugai, G., & Colvin, G. (1998). Reducing problem behavior through a school-wide system of effective behavioral support: Investigation of a school-wide social skills training program and contextual interventions. *School Psychology Review, 27,* 446–459.

Maccoby, E. (1998). *The two sexes: Growing up apart, coming together.* Cambridge, MA: Harvard University Press.

Maines, B., & Robinson, G. (1998). The no blame approach to bullying. In D. Shorrocks-Taylor (Ed.), *Directions in educational psychology* (pp. 281–295). London: Whurr.

Marshall, D. (2006). Safe and healthy sports environments. In H. Frumkin, R. J. Geller, I. L. Rubin, & J. Nodvin (Eds.), *Safe and healthy school environments* (pp. 238–247). New York: Oxford University Press.

McDougal, J. L., Clonan, S. M., & Martens, B. K. (2000). Using organizational change procedures to promote the acceptability of prereferral intervention services: The school-based intervention team project. *School Psychology Quarterly, 15,* 149–171.

Merrell, K. W., Gueldner, B. A., & Tran, O. K. (2008). Social and emotional learning: A school-wide approach to intervention for socialization, friendship problems, and more. In B. Doll and J. Cummings (Eds.), *Transforming school mental health services: Population-based approaches to promoting the competency and wellness of children* (pp. 165–186). Thousand Oaks, CA: Corwin Press in cooperation with the National Association of School Psychologists.

Moore, R. (2006). Playgrounds: The 150 year old model. In H. Frumkin, R. J. Geller, I. L. Rubin, & J. Nodvin (Eds.), *Safe and healthy school environments* (pp. 86–103). New York: Oxford University Press.

Murphy, H. A., Hutchinson, J. M., & Bailey, J. S. (1983). Behavioral school psychology goes outdoors: The effect of organized games on playground aggression. *Journal of Applied Behavior Analysis, 16,* 29–35.

Murphy, P. (2002). The effect of classroom meetings on the reduction of recess problems: A single case design. Unpublished doctoral dissertation, University of Denver.

National Center for Education Statistics. (2007). *Public use data files and documentations: Foods and physical activity in public schools 2005.* Washington, DC: Author.

National Recreation and Park Association. (2008). *The dirty dozen: 12 playground hazards.* Downloaded December 12, 2008, from www.nrpa.org

National Research Council and the Institute of Medicine. (2004). *Engaging schools: Fostering high school students' motivation to learn.* Committee on Increasing High School Students' Engagement and Motivation to Learn; Board on Children, Youth, and Families; Division of Behavioral and Social Sciences and Education. Washington, DC: National Academies Press.

Olweus, D. (1991). Bully/victim problems among school children: Basic facts and effects of a school based intervention program. In I. Rubin & D. Pepler (Eds.), *The development and treatment of childhood aggression.* Hillsdale, NJ: Erlbaum.

Olweus, D., Limber, S. P., & Mihalic, S. (1999). *The bullying prevention program: Blueprints for violence prevention, Vol. 10.* Boulder, CO: Center for the Study and Prevention of Violence.

Parten, M. (1932). Social participation among preschool children. *Journal of Abnormal and Social Psychology, 27,* 243–269.

Pellegrini, A. D. (1984). The social cognitive ecology of preschool classrooms. *International Journal of Behavioral Development, 7,* 321–332.

Pellegrini, A. D. (1995). *School recess and playground behavior: Educational and developmental roles.* Albany: State University of New York Press.

Pellegrini, A. D. (2005). *Recess: Its role in education and development.* Mahwah, NJ: Lawrence Erlbaum.

Pellegrini, A. D., & Bartini, M. (2000). A longitudinal study of bullying, victimization, and peer affiliation during the transition from primary school to middle school. *American Educational Research Journal, 37,* 699–725.

Pellegrini, A. D., & Blatchford, P. (2000). *The child at school: Interactions with peers and teachers.* New York: Oxford University Press.

Pellegrini, A. D., Blatchford, P., Kato, K., & Baines, E. (2004). A short-term longitudinal study of children's playground games in primary school: Implications for adjustment to school and social adjustment in the USA and the UK. *Social Development, 13,* 107–123.

Pellegrini, A. D., & Bohn, C. M. (2005). The role of recess in children's cognitive performance and school adjustment. *Educational Researcher, 34*, 13–19.

Pellegrini, A. D., Kato, K., Blatchford, P., & Baines, E. (2002). A short-term longitudinal study of children's playground games across the first year of school: Implications for social competence and adjustment to school. *American Educational Research Journal, 39*, 991–1015.

Pellegrini, A. D., & Smith, P. K. (1998). Physical activity play: The nature and function of a neglected aspect of play. *Child Development, 69*, 577–598.

Roderick, C., Pitchford, M., & Miller, A. (1997). Reducing aggressive playground behaviour by means of a school-wide raffle. *Educational Psychology in Practice, 13*, 57–63.

Rubin, K., Fein, G., & Vendenberg, B. (1983). Play. In E. M. Hetherington (Ed.), *Handbook of child psychology, socialization, personality and social development* (Vol. 4, pp. 693–774). New York: Wiley.

Santa, A. (2007). The playground as classroom. *Educational Leadership, 64*(8), 78–79.

Schoen, S. F., & Bullard, M. (2002). Action research during recess: A time for children with autism to play and learn. *Teaching Exceptional Children, 35*, 36–39.

Shure, M. B. (1997). Interpersonal cognitive problem solving: Primary prevention of early high-risk behaviors in the preschool and primary years. In G. Albee, & T. Gullotta (Eds.), *Primary prevention works* (pp. 167–188). Thousand Oaks, CA: Sage Publications.

Siemers, E. (2006). *Children's aggression at recess: Examining the relationship between the playground environment, aggressive behavior, and reports of worry.* Unpublished doctoral dissertation, University of Nebraska–Lincoln.

Swearer, S. M., & Doll, B. (2002). Bullying in schools: An ecological framework. In R. A. Geffner, M. T. Loring, & C. Young (Eds.), *Bullying behavior: Current issues, research and interventions.* Binghamton, NY: Haworth.

Tinsworth, D., & McDonald, J. (2001). *Special study: Injuries and deaths associated with children's playground equipment.* Bethesda, MD: U.S. Consumer Product Safety Commission.

Todd, A., Haugen, T., Anderson, K., & Spriggs, M. (2002). Teaching recess: Low-cost efforts producing effective results. *Journal of Positive Behavior Interventions, 4*, 46–52.

Truscott, S. D., Cosgrove, G., Meyers, J., & Eidel-Barkman, K. A. (2000). The acceptability of organizational consultation with prereferral intervention teams. *School Psychology Quarterly, 15*, 172–206.

United Nations. (1989). *Convention on the rights of the child* (General Assembly Resolution 44/25). New York: United Nations.

United Nations. (1991). U.N. Convention on the rights of the child: Unofficial summary of articles. *School Psychology Review, 20*, 339–343.

U.S. Consumer Product Safety Commission. (2008, April). *Public playground safety handbook*. Retrieved December 12, 2008, from www.cpsc.gov

Waters, E., & Sroufe, L. (1983). Social competence as a developmental construct. *Developmental Review, 3*, 79–97.

Webster's desk dictionary of the English language. (1983). New York: Gramercy.

Zajac, R. J., & Hartup, W. W. (1997). Friends as coworkers: Research review and classroom implications. *The Elementary School Journal, 98*, 3–13.

Index

Rules
  of conduct
    aggression issues, 14–15
    ClassMaps Survey data
      distortion, 45
    physical facility
      limitations and, 26
  decision (interpretation of
    ClassMaps data), 43, 45
  of games
    games and, 21, 23
    revising for safety, 32–33
    student establishment of,
      84–85

S

Safety checklist, 103–104
Safety issues
  physical facility guidelines,
    28–29
  physically intense games
    and, 32–33
  resources, 99–100
Self-regulated play, 1
Skills, social, 8
Social competence; *See*
    Competence, social
Social interactions, 1
Social isolation; *See* Isolation,
    social
Social learning, 142–148
Social networks, 7
Social reinforcement, 7
Social responses, menu of
    options, 8
Social status, 12
Social structures, 12–13
Social values, 89–90
Solitary play, 20
Space, physical facility
    guidelines, 27, 28
Spontaneity, characteristics
    of socially competent
    students, 8
Staircase programs, 62
Strategies, play, 20
Stresses, social, 9
Strong Kids program, 69

Structural repairs, 33
Structure, classroom meetings,
    46
Student-supervisor ratio, 35
Supervision, 2
  checklist, 105–106
  interventions; *See*
    Interventions
  physical facility guidelines,
    27
  playground facilities, 34–36
Surfacing material, physical
    facility guidelines, 28
Symbolic play, 21

T

Taunts, 16–17
Teaching new social behavior, 7
Teasing, 54
  case example, 81–88
  verbal aggression, 16–17
Teasing Form, 82, 84, 115
Teasing graph, 85, 87
Teasing Thermometer, 85, 87,
    117
Theory of change, 7
Timing, interventions
    promoting social
    competence, 61–62
Toddler and preschool years,
    friendships of, 9–10
Training, bullying prevention
    programs, 65–66
Tripping injuries, 28
Tutors, friends as, 9

U

UCLA Center for Mental Health
    Services in the Schools,
    70
Understanding, Parents
    Friendship Meeting
    parent information
    curriculum, 142–148
Unstructured settings,
    aggression in, 16

CD Contents:
Practical Resources

ClassMaps Survey 2007
Empty ClassMaps PowerPoint Graphs
Parents' Friendship Meeting Handbook
Plan for Change Form
Playground Safety Checklist
Playground Supervision Checklist
PowerPoint: Fostering Social Competence
PowerPoint: Playground Supervision
PowerPoint: Resilient Playgrounds
Promoting Playground Play Checklist
Teasing Form
Teasing Thermometer